YORKSHIRE

LIVES & LANDSCAPES

By the same author

Poetry
Doodles in the Margins of my Life
Swallows Return
Three Brontë Poems
Pirouette of Earth: a Novel in Verse
Natural Light
Messages from Distant Shores

Prose Poems
The Comet of 1811
The Snake and the Star

Literary Criticism
Pilgrims from Loneliness: an interpretation of Charlotte Brontë's
Jane Eyre *and* Villette

YORKSHIRE

LIVES & LANDSCAPES

IAN M. EMBERSON

SUTTON PUBLISHING

First published in 2006 by
Sutton Publishing Limited · Phoenix Mill
Thrupp · Stroud · Gloucestershire · GL5 2BU

British Library Cataloguing in Publication Data
A catalogue record for this book is available from the British Library.

ISBN 0-7509-4466-8

*For Ken Edward Smith who once had the kindness
to describe the author as 'an honorary Yorkshireman'.*

Typeset in 10.5/13pt Galliard.
Typesetting and origination by
Sutton Publishing Limited.
Printed and bound in England by
J.H. Haynes & Co. Ltd, Sparkford.

Contents

Acknowledgements

Many people have been generous with their time in assisting me with this book. My thanks to them are very sincere even if I only mention them in this brief alphabetical list as follows:

Bohuslav Barlow, Roger Birch, the staff of the Brontë Parsonage Museum, Calderdale Council Community Services (Libraries, Museums and Arts), Debjani Chatterjee, Sue Clough, Mark Croft, Bob Duckett, Hermant Dutta, Gordon Dyson, Edward and Helen Gaunt, Huddersfield Choral Social – especially Bob Edwards and Malcolm Hinchcliffe, the staff of the *Huddersfield Examiner*, Horace Kirk, Kirklees Council Culture and Leisure Services, Barbara Lightowler, Richard Littlewood, Mary Lord, the Mehta family, Anthony Mellor, Mark Murphy, David Quirke, John Richardson, Peter Sanson, Sheeran Lock Ltd, Michael Smith and Steve Sneyd.

And finally thanks are due to my wife Catherine, who has helped me so much with the big things in life – as well as its trivialities.

The author, Catherine and Sooty.
(Photograph: Roy Kirk)

About the Author

Ian Emberson was born in 1936 at Hove in Sussex, and is proud to have been christened by the poet Andrew Young. His mother was a gardener's daughter who had been brought up in the village of Alloway in Ayrshire, where Robert Burns was born. His father was a journalist from Essex. Ian took to painting and writing in early childhood, and has pursued these activities on and off ever since.

During his National Service Ian was in the Royal Signals, serving in Cyprus between 1955 and 1957. Since then he has earned a living both in horticulture and librarianship, before taking early retirement in 1986 to concentrate on painting and writing. His publications include six books of poetry and two of prose-poems, as well as numerous articles. In 1996 Bradford Playhouse produced his one-actor play *Cockerel Crowing Dawn*, based on the life of the Russian composer Mussorgsky. Ian also wrote the libretto for Daniel Bath's opera *The Forest*, first performed at the Hebden Bridge Festival in 2003. Four other composers have set his poetry to music: Peter Copley, John Bartlett, Gordon Dyson and Robin Terry.

Ian met his wife Catherine through the Brontë Society, and together they have worked on various pieces of research. One of these led to the discovery of George Sowden's *Recollections of the Brontës*, which had lain virtually forgotten for over a hundred years but was finally published in 2005. In the same year the Brontë Society published Ian's book *Pilgrims from Loneliness: An Interpretation of Charlotte Brontë's* Jane Eyre *and* Villette.

Ian lives in Yorkshire with his wife Catherine and Sooty the dog.

The author, Ian M. Emberson, 2006.
(Photograph: Roger Birch)

Mrs Smailes? One of the curious statues by James Woodford on either side of the entrance to Huddersfield Central Library. Despite contrary opinions, it represents the Spirit of Art listening to the whispering voices of Inspiration. (Author's collection)

1

The Town (Huddersfield)

3 August 1994 – a day of low cloud and rain. I am alone in the living room of our home at Todmorden in Yorkshire – alone that is, with the exception of our mongrel Sooty, so christened because he was born soot-black, although he soon developed large areas of white and tan, making his name a subject for embarrassed explanation. Catherine, my girlfriend of six years, is no doubt now slaving at her job at the bank, keeping the customers happy, the boss happy, herself happy (an almost impossible task in these times of competitive strain), while I sprawl on the sofa in the decadent luxury of early retirement.

The large rectangular picture-window in this room frames a fine view of the Upper Calder Valley. Below the grey rain-clouds, the furthest object is the edge of the Pennines, a stretch going by the name of Langfield Moor. It is a flat-topped area, and the horizon is punctuated by two rocky craters, which are the remains of ancient quarries, and the sloping sides are lined with dry-stone walls. Lower down is West Longfield Farm, with the surrounding fields forming a wavy ribbon of vivid green, between the duller greens above and below. In the foreground there is a rough patch of wilderness, at present covered with ragwort, rosebay willow herb and convolvulus, leading down to the railway line which follows the valley up from Halifax, and at this point divides (as does the valley itself), the branches going north-west and south-west respectively, and over the border into Lancashire.

Today at last I feel in a mood to tackle something which has been in my mind for some while – to write an autobiography, or at least a fragment of one. But autobiography is a frightening word. One thinks of the many impediments: the episodes in life one is somewhat ashamed of; the people one might offend. Furthermore there is the question as to what really is a true autobiography – is it the tidy respectable version that goes into a CV or a job application (even these documents require some skill as a fiction-writer, as most of their compilers know), or is it the more intimate story one might tell one's friends? Deeper still, does it include all those things known only to oneself – the secret hopes, fears and desires that one might hesitate to reveal even to the person dearest to you. And may there be an even deeper level – a story not fully recognised even by oneself?

However, much of the above is irrelevant, since what I have in mind is somewhat different. Rather than make myself the hero of the piece, and thereby elevate my trivial ups and downs to a grandeur they do not warrant, I want to make Yorkshire itself my hero, with the moors, the valleys, the big industrial towns, the small stone-built villages. But more than the place itself, the people and the culture of the people – their music, their art, their writings. No doubt such an attempt by an individual (and a comer-in at that) will be a hotchpotch, fragmentary and extremely subjective. Be that as it may, I intend to make the attempt. And my own role will be that of a solitary figure in a landscape painting, there merely to convey the feeling that someone sees what is around them.

My first introduction to Yorkshire was by no means auspicious. I was 18 at the time, and my visit consisted of a month's 'square bashing' at Catterick Camp, as an introduction to National Service. The year was 1955, and it was one of the coldest Februarys on record. I can hardly say that I saw the soil of Yorkshire, as it was continually covered with a screen of whiteness. On my first day in the army I can remember running from Richmond station (Richmond in Yorkshire, of course) to catch the dilapidated charabanc that was to take us to Catterick. After a few miles a grim and massive building loomed ahead amid the predominant white – it was like a Siberian prison. 'Right lads, that's your camp,' the driver muttered.

Of the next few weeks I retain various vague memories, such as the pair of dirty bedraggled swans which were kept by the edge of the parade ground as mascots (for what reason I can't imagine). I also recollect the stretch of dreary, sodden moorland where we did our rifle practice. From the barrack-room window we seemed to look out over miles and miles of uniform snow, but there was one dominant hill, high but flat-topped. Was it High Harter Hill? I still don't know, for none of my subsequent experiences of the area tally with those distant memories.

My second brief visit was in the summer of 1962, and consisted of a fortnight's practical experience at Sheffield Public Library as part of my librarianship course. I well remember the enthusiasm of the staff, whose library system was then one of the finest in the country – and may be still for all I know. The first day off I had was devoted to a visit to the Brontë Parsonage at Haworth. It was to be the first of many. I also recollect a young girl named Carlean, with whom I explored the slums of Tinsley and Attercliffe, and rambled on the local heather-clad moors.

Nine years later I returned again to Yorkshire, but not this time for a month or a fortnight, but, as it turned out, for the rest of my life. It was a January evening in 1971, and it was dark and miserable, with lines of traffic and unfamiliar road signs reflected in the puddles; this strange, almost hostile, environment was my first impression of Huddersfield. Like every driver to an unknown place, I looked first for a car park, and found one beneath a modern but drab civic building. I made my first human contact, with the car park attendant, and asked if he could recommend a hotel. He mentioned The Queen (now the Sole Mio Restaurant), where I booked in, and then went in search of a meal. In Cloth Hall Street I found a Wimpey Bar, and had a mixed grill (in those days I was not a vegetarian). The waitress was an Irish girl, plain but very pleasant, and there was something reassuring about the way she served me. I later discovered her name was Barbara. When, some years later, she changed her place of work, I promptly changed my place of eating, so that her agreeable smile as she handed me my cups of tea was a recurring delight for many years.

Hammond's Yard still retains its old-fashioned charm, despite modernisation. (Author's collection)

Next morning I went into Menzies Bookshop and bought Tolstoy's *War and Peace* in two paperback volumes. It was a wise choice, as there were many lonely evenings ahead. Then I wandered around the centre of town, looking with especial interest at the Central Library, where, later that afternoon, I had a job interview for the post of Music Librarian. It was so unobtrusively labelled that I had a problem working out that this curious art-deco fabrication really was the place itself. Far more intrusive than the small diagonal signs saying 'Public Library' were two gigantic pseudo-Egyptian statues, their hands held in odd positions (like a library assistant gesturing that a ticket was lost). I later heard an anecdote about a school class, who, at the time of its opening, had to write an essay describing the new library. One little girl started off: 'The new Huddersfield Public Library was opened on October 29th 1937 by Councillor and Mrs Thomas Smailes, and their statues appear on either side of the entrance.'

The interview that afternoon proved not too much of an ordeal. I remember the moment when my new chief, Stanley Dibnah, shook my hand and said 'Welcome to the staff, Mr Emberson', as a sort of new beginning in life. I recollect my eye going to the window, and looking at the rows of soot-stained mill chimneys which were still a feature of the town centre, and realising that this area was now to be my home. As if reading my thoughts, Mr Dibnah said: 'Oh, it's not as bad as it used to be – not now they've made it smokeless.'

Huddersfield at that time was having the final fling in an orgy of demolition. While the nearby town of Halifax had the good sense to preserve its magnificent nineteenth-century buildings, Huddersfield ruthlessly pulled down the Cloth Hall, the Market Hall and much else. At the Packhorse Inn, a few days before its destruction, they had a dinner to celebrate, an event that was later commemorated in my friend Gordon Dyson's poem 'Demolishing the Demolition Dinner'. (Alas, the poem itself seems to have been likewise demolished, as I can trace no surviving copy.) There was even talk of pulling down the magnificent Town Hall, and it took the intervention of Sir John Barbirolli himself to save it. In fact at this time one might have been excused for thinking that an intensive bombing raid had recently swept through the town, the resulting 'bomb-sites' being pressed into use as vast sprawling car parks. Gradually the blanks became filled with new structures, most of them undistinguished, except for the covered market and the Midland Bank building in Cloth Hall Street. Soon the only way to get an impression of nineteenth-century Huddersfield was to glance up some of the intriguing old back yards, especially those off King Street – Goldthorpe's Yard, Hammond's Yard and Wormald's Yard.*

Having secured my job, the next thing was to find a place to stay. I booked in at the towering YMCA building, and was allocated room 19. The first evening I spent alone in my new abode drawing the view from the window – in which the Leeds Road gasometers were the predominant feature. Of the short walk to work next morning I remember only the screaming of innumerable starlings as I crossed St Peter's churchyard. The first day at work was the usual whirl of meeting countless new faces, both staff and public. I had been through it all before. In the first half of my career I had had nine jobs, four in horticulture and five in librarianship. Perhaps I thought of the Huddersfield post as just another one, to last for a few years. In fact it stretched to the end of my working life.

There were various mundane matters to be attended to over the next few days, such as establishing links with a local barber. I chose the small shop of George Hulme, just round the corner from the YMCA. George was a gentleman of the old school in most matters, including haircuts. However, he made a few concessions to his 'short back and sides' tradition, in order to curry favour with local poets, artists and eccentrics like myself. When trade was slack and the shop was quiet George would hold forth about some of Huddersfield's famous characters. He remembered many such legendary beings: one was an old man nicknamed 'Maritana', because he was always singing songs from Vincent Wallace's once-famous opera; another was a young man whose behaviour most of the time was quite normal, but who would suddenly be seized with the delusion that he had turned into a railway engine. Thus, when strolling along the street with his lady-friend, he would abruptly start emitting hoots, whistles and puffs; his arms started flailing around, and he would then charge off in imitation of the *Flying Scotsman*. The lady apparently took these attacks quite calmly, remarking to her friends, 'Don't worry, he'll be back in time.' Another anecdote concerned a gentleman who drove up to a local hostelry and went in for refreshment, leaving his horse and cart outside. While he consumed large quantities of ale within, his 'friends' unharnessed the horse, threaded the cart shafts through some iron railings, reharnessed the horse to the now-immobile cart, and then hid to watch his consternation when he finally emerged.

* See L. Browning and R.K. Senior, *The Old Yards of Huddersfield* (Huddersfield Civic Society, 1986).

One problem with the buildings of a new town is the question of which entrance you use, and what exactly you do when you get inside. I have always been a keen swimmer, and usually go to the pool of any town I visit. No two pools are the same as regards customs and traditions, and mastering the mysteries of one is no help whatever in visiting another. Practices differ even in the matter of to which part of your anatomy you attach the key to the clothes locker. At some pools the band to which the key is attached is narrow and calculated to fit on the wrist; at others it is wider and more suited to the ankle. Attempts to defy tradition result either in cutting off your circulation or in seeing the wretched thing fall off and sink to the bottom of the pool. I usually ask about such matters when I first go in. On my first visit to Cambridge Road Baths, however, I decided to use a different approach, and merely followed the example of some small boys who had gone in just ahead of me. Alas, I was unaware that there were separate pools for adults and children. After I'd been swimming around for a few minutes, one of the young lady attendants leant over the side and asked if I'd mind getting out of the kiddies' pool!

I had a somewhat similar experience on the evening of this self-same day. There was a concert at Huddersfield Town Hall, a somewhat unusual event in that the Choral Society and the Philharmonic Society had joined forces for it. To the untutored eye it seems obvious that the way for the audience to get into the Town Hall is via the imposing entrance in Ramsden Street. However, as I later discovered, this door is mainly used by council staff, and the entrances for concert-goers are in Princess Street and Corporation Street. Unaware of this, I strode in briskly from Ramsden Street and marched up the magnificent staircase beneath Giovanni Grignashi's copy of Leonardo's *Last Supper*. I must admit I was a bit disconcerted when I found myself pushing a path through the bow-tied males and pink-dressed females of the Choral Society, and even more surprised when I pushed open a door and found myself emerging from beneath the stage of the main concert hall!

However, once I found my seat all was well. For a few minutes I glanced around at that vast temple of music (designed by John Abbey and opened in 1881), admiring the dazzling chandeliers and the heads of the Greek gods and goddesses looking down at me,* the gilded angels with their trumpets, the scallop-shell design above the console, and even the row of brash poinsettias, set off by green ferns, lining the front of the stage. There are always some wonderful moments before a concert, and this was no exception as the oboe sounded its 'A', the orchestra tuned up and applause greeted the leader.

At last the dapper figure of Arthur Butterworth (a noted composer as well as a conductor) appeared on the rostrum, raised his baton and then that restless repetitive pattern on the strings sounded, before the chorus burst in with: 'Zadok the priest, and Nathan the prophet, anointed Solomon King . . .'. In the second half choir and orchestra again joined forces, this time for Beethoven's *Choral Symphony*. I remember little of the performance but I do recall the remark of a little old lady to her friend as we all went out of the (correct) door: 'Eh, there were too much banging on't drums fer my liking'.

* See David Hammond's article, 'Making headway with the gods', *Huddersfield Examiner*, 23 October 1990, p. 10.

The Library

One might assume that a library was at its busiest at such times as a Saturday afternoon, especially during the crescendo which usually gathers momentum just before closing time. It is then that with aching arms the 'Saturday girls' heave the last batch of 'light' romances back on to the shelves (the 'light' refers to the content, not the weight), the gentleman in charge of the Lending Department announces in as booming a voice as he can command, 'We're closing in five minutes', and every assistant looks at the clock longing for those minutes to pass. It is at such times that the vagaries of fate and human wilfulness impel an elderly lady to enter the Music Library, and insist on starting the Linguaphone Arabic course. Attempts to put her off until Monday morning are unavailing – no, she must commence her studies that very afternoon. So she is initiated into the strange rules and regulations governing the borrowing thereof, while the janitor stands in the doorway viciously jangling his keys.

But it is not at these moments that the real life of the library progresses; it is rather at such times as the very late evening, when the only activity in the building itself is the night-cleaner playing darts by himself in the deserted staff-room. Then the real purpose of the place finds fruition: on the turntables in homes all around the town Kathleen Ferrier will be singing 'My Boy Willie' above the clicks and groove-wear left by the many previous borrowers (I speak of the unenlightened times before the invention of CDs), choirs will be mumbling along as they clutch their tatty copies of 'Olivet to Calvary', and ancient ladies will be drooling through thin lips over the latest production by Mills & Boon (assuming it's a library that stocks them).

'A good book is the precious life-blood of a master spirit', wrote John Milton, and one might suppose that library assistants, being surrounded by all these flowerings of culture, would live on a very high spiritual and intellectual plane. Alas, this is not so, since most of their time is devoted to the most abject trivialities. The basic fact about a public library is that things are borrowed. The librarian's main job is therefore twofold: to keep track of who has borrowed what, and to make sure that it eventually comes back – preferably on time. Various devices have been invented to help with these duties. The method used almost universally when I entered the profession was the Browne system. This involved a ticket representing a particular book, and a pocket-shaped piece of card representing the borrower. When the book went out, the book ticket was inserted into the borrower's card, and this happy union was known as a charge. Filed in order under the date of return, it served as a true record of the transaction until the item came back. But, like all human activities,

Huddersfield Central Library was designed by E.H. Ashburner and opened in 1940.
(Author's collection)

this well-devised scheme was subject to mishap. An assistant would seize the wrong ticket when a book was returned, or a tray of charges would be knocked on the floor and futile attempts would have to be made to marry up the fragments to their correct partners. Errors such as these could result in that most dreaded phenomenon – 'the crossed ticket'. Some members of the public would take such mishaps good-humouredly. Thus the elderly gentleman from the Choral Society whose ticket got mixed up with that of the gorgeous female next door would be teased mercilessly amid innuendos of extra-marital relationships. But the old maid bombarded with overdue reminders for *Sex and the Single Woman* was less easily placated.

Outsiders might suppose that the Music Library was a haven of peace exempt from such petty annoyances – but this was far from the case. Fond as I am of the old-fashioned long-playing gramophone record, it was prey to many ills. Players with a damaged or worn-out stylus caused groove wear, and the slightest carelessness in handling resulted in scratches, while various fluids, such as tea, coffee and wine, somehow found their way on to the surfaces. Every disc was then accompanied by charts, one for each side, on which the history of all these mishaps could be recorded; the marks were stamped with the library stamp, and their position referred to by the hour hand of a clock. Thus Beethoven's *Fifth Symphony* might have a scratch at three o'clock (one hoped it coincided with the loudest passage), and Elizabeth Schwarzkopf's operetta highlights had groove wear on band four (almost certainly 'the best bit').

Sets of orchestral parts also had their own peculiar problems. Many were old and seldom used, and one tended to take it on trust that what was said on the label coincided with the contents. On one occasion the Huddersfield Philharmonic borrowed a set of Tchaikovsky's *1812 Overture*. A short way into the rehearsal it became obvious that something was wrong. When the players examined their scores more closely, it transpired that some of them were playing the work as Tchaikovsky originally wrote it, while others were performing an arrangement. The result was even closer to the tumult of battle than the composer had intended.

Most of the enquiries in a music library are fairly predictable. Questions about music theory are very rare, although I was once asked to explain what a chord of the thirteenth was – and failed to do so. The majority are of the 'Who wrote the Moonlight Sonata, and where can I find it?' variety. There are also such things as 'Have you got . . . ?', with the gap being filled in with a rendition of the big theme. I even had people singing pieces down the telephone at me. All this was quite routine, and it is only the more unusual ones that have lingered in my memory. I think I had been in the job for about a week when two folk singers named Judith and Pamela came to me one evening with a problem. They were due to sing at Morpeth in Northumberland the following weekend, and had realised with horror that they didn't know any Northumbrian folksongs. A search of the shelves was unavailing, but I told them that I knew 'Cullercoats Bay' (my previous post having been at nearby Tynemouth). Pamela immediately asked me to sing it. This was a bit daunting – singing was definitely not my forte (in fact I had been thrown out of the descant group at school). Fortunately the place was quiet, so I closed the Music Library doors and gave one of my very rare performances, while Pamela copied it down, both words and music. I gather they duly sang it at Morpeth, and it was well received.

Because you are in the public eye, people seem to think they can ask about any topic whatever. I once had a young girl come up to the counter, and shyly ask if she could have my advice on something. Of course I agreed. She then told me she was trying to join the army, but had failed the medical because she had a scar on her midriff. What should she do about it? She then hitched up her pullover, and displayed the scar for my inspection. I can't now remember what advice I gave her – but I certainly felt it lay somewhat beyond my duties as a librarian.

Since the art books were shelved in the Music Library, I often found myself dealing with art enquiries as well. These were mostly routine. One question, however, lay midway between the two art forms. It came from a lady of eccentric dress and habits. She told me she had painted an illustration to Rimsky-Korsakov's opera *Snegurochka* ('The Snow Maiden'), and would I like to see it? Again I naively said 'yes', and forgot all about it. The following afternoon I saw the lady entering the Music Library, clutching under her arm what I at first took to be a roll of carpet. This she laid on the floor and unrolled, and behold – her illustration to *Snegurochka*! It was painted on a piece of wrapping paper, and was so large that people entering and leaving the library had to stride over it. Of its artistic merits I can only say that if the technique had been equal to the powers of imagination it would have been a masterpiece!

The Village (Thurstonland)

My first awareness of the village of Thurstonland was a sort of subconscious expectation. Ever since childhood, when left with a pencil or crayon and a few moments to while away, I have drawn the same doodle – a clump of trees with a church spire sticking out of the top. Psychiatrists may make of that what they will, but there it is. A few weeks into my time at Huddersfield I had a more tangible presentiment of the place. In Brian Turner's estate agents I picked up the details of a house, and saw that magical name 'Thurstonland'. It had the feeling of a little kingdom all on its own, definitely not a part of the British Empire, but a land set apart – where the rules and regulations frustrating the lives of the rest of humankind had no influence. Brian's mother, noticing my interest, remarked: 'You'll be right away in the woods and fields there'. The fact that her words echoed one of my favourite pieces of music, Smetana's 'From Bohemia's Woods and Fields', increased my curiosity even further, and I got into my car without further ado. And then suddenly there it was! Rounding the crest of the hill beyond Farnley Tyas I realised that my childish doodle had been made flesh: in the shallow dip below me stood the clump of trees, mostly sycamore and ash, and in their midst rose the slender Victorian Gothic spire of St Thomas's Church. Needless to say I bought the house, and lived in it for the next twenty-three years.

The position of Thurstonland is best understood when you look east from the Pennines around Black Hill. There in the grey-blue distance are two low hills, and between them a long saddle, with a sharp spike at the centre. On closer inspection the spike resolves itself into the church spire, lying just east of the ridge of the saddle. Below that saddle lies the steep west-facing scar slope, commanding a wonderful view across the woods and meadows of the Holme Valley. The gentler dipped slope stretches to the east, its small fields separated by a medley of dry-stone walls and hawthorn hedges. The fairly sharp hill to the south is Pike Stye, and the climb to its summit became one of my favourite walks. The flat-topped eminence to the north doesn't appear to have a designation, but it is crowned by a copse of fine beech trees with the curious name of Farnley Plump.

In addition to the church, Thurstonland has all those things a good village should have: a pub, a village green, a war memorial, a few farms, houses old and new, and football and cricket pitches – traditionally the highest in Yorkshire. Most of the houses cluster along the main street, and many of the older ones boast rows of upstairs mullioned windows, which once shed precious light on the busy activities of hand-loom weavers. Two farms lie close to the village, while others (mostly small) are scattered around it. The fields likewise are small, except where several little fields have merged into one big one. Dotted among the fields are patches of woodland with such names as Clough Wood, Round Wood and Black Gutters. And far beneath the village the Huddersfield to Sheffield railway delves a way through, darkly and deeply, its course being punctuated by three air shafts. I remember I was once picking blackberries near one of these shafts in the company of some children, and could hardly believe my ears when I distinctly heard the sound of a train rushing towards me. The children carried on picking unconcernedly, while I stood listening anxiously to its approach – until it roared by in the tunnel far below.

Thurstonland. The very name itself was part of the attraction for me, and it is also a clue to its early history. There are other similar names in the area, notably Thurgoland (on the Huddersfield–Sheffield road) and Thurlstone near Penistone. Most of the place-names beginning with 'Th' originated with the Danish invasion, although a few are Anglo-Saxon. I don't know for certain the origin of

Thurstonland church on a snowy day. (Author's collection)

The Rose and Crown public house, Thurstonland. (Author's collection)

Thurstonland, but Thurgoland derives from Thorger's land,* so by analogy there was presumably a great Dane called Thurston or Thornstein or some such name, who coveted this stretch of land, eventually acquired it and gave it his name. The name can cause confusion when studying early records, for it referred not only to what we now think of as the village, but also to the township of Thurstonland, which embraced a much wider area, stretching from Storthes Hall to Brockholes.

The area merited a mention in the Domesday Book, and two hundred years later John, 7th Earl Warren, is also referred to as the Lord of Thurstonland. In about 1345 it was given as a grange to the Abbey of Roche near Maltby,** and it stayed in the monks' possession until the dissolution of the monasteries in 1540, when Henry VIII gave it to a gentleman with the somewhat earthy name John Storthes of Shittylington. It only stayed with the Storthes family for about sixty years, but their name persists to this day in Storthes Hall, a former mental hospital that is now used as student accommodation for the University of Huddersfield. In about 1603 the estate passed to the Horsfall family, who originally came from Mankinholes near Todmorden. Eventually much of the area to the west became part of the Dartmouth Estate.

Of course agriculture was the main source of livelihood, supplemented by weaving – as evinced by the weavers' cottages along the village street. In the early nineteenth century many villagers found employment in the mills at Brockholes, while later the quarry and brickworks in the area known as 'Top o' th' Bank' were both sources of work.

* Readers' Digest, *Atlas*, p. 208.
** Hammerton, J.A. (ed.), *Wonderful Britain*, 4 vols (Fleetway House, no date), vol. 1, p. 205.

The religious history of Thurstonland is somewhat curious. In 1808 a chapel was completed in what is now the south-east corner of the present churchyard. The money for this was provided by three groups, the Methodists, the Independents and the Anglicans, and all of them used the building at fixed times. However, this harmonious state of affairs, like most such idylls, did not last long. Disputes soon broke out, and had reached such a pitch by the early 1830s that the Constables had to be called in to prevent Sunday morning riots. Eventually, in 1836, the Methodists built their own chapel, and left the Anglicans in sole command (what happened to the Independents I have no idea). The new chapel was, however, too small, and on 26 July 1869 the Countess of Dartmouth laid the foundation stone of the present church. It is pleasing to learn that this event was followed by a massive public luncheon, which was consumed in a large tent specially erected for the purpose.

By the time I knew it Thurstonland had become mainly a dormitory village. Many of the inhabitants would be engaged during the day in making tractors at Meltham or gears at David Brown's at Huddersfield, or in countless other industries and services. The village for them, as for myself, was the place of refuge to which one hastened after a weary day; a place for walks, sport and gardening during the long weekends. But there were of course some who lived and worked in the village. One such was a

Fred Haigh, aged 8, feeding pigs on a farm near Thurstonland in the 1930s. (Courtesy of Edward and Helen Gaunt)

Edward Gaunt feeding sheep at
West View near Thurstonland.
(Author's collection)

gentleman who lived in a cottage on the slopes of Pike Stye, and still earned a living by the ancient craft of hand-loom weaving. Although he borrowed records from the Music Library, I cannot now remember his name, but I recollect his appearance. He was quite young, blond and fresh-faced, yet he seemed somehow older than the oldest man in the place. I never visited his home, and can only imagine the quaint activity of this twentieth-century follower of Timmy Feather.* Shortly after my arrival, for some reason he shifted to the Dorset–Hampshire border, there to continue his traditional calling.

There were plenty of anecdotes about bygone days when Thurstonland was more of a self-sufficient community. Old Mr Charlesworth, who delivered our newspapers, would often reminisce about his boyhood. He seems then to have had a penchant for pretending that things long-since defunct were still in action. The tall chimney of the brickworks had been smokeless for many years when he and some other boys, bent on a bit of harmless mischief, gathered all the old boxes and paper they could find, put them at the bottom of the chimney and set fire to the lot. Great was the amazement of the villagers at seeing this extinct industry suddenly bursting into activity.

A similar tale concerned an old tractor which had lain rusting near the main village street for a long time. Despite its decrepitude, the boys discovered that one of its parts was still in working order – namely the hooter. They therefore tied a very long piece of string to the lever that worked this device, retreated as far as the string would permit and then lay in wait until some unfortunate passer-by approached –

* See Whiteley Turner, *A Spring-time Saunter Round and About Brontë Land*, 3rd edn (Halifax Courier, 1913, reprinted by Rigg, 1986).

and then enjoyed the sight of the person's consternation when the tractor suddenly bellowed forth its unholy blast.

The great love which the inhabitants had for the village was the subject of another tale. It seems that a young man had decided to emigrate to Canada. Having settled his affairs and said goodbye to all his friends, he set off on his great adventure. However, when he reached the old signpost at the edge of Farnley Moor he paused to take a last look at his former home. There it was below him – the church, the woods, the fields, the familiar playgrounds of his boyhood. He looked for a long time, and then apparently muttered (in words that suggest he was a reader of Robert Burns): 'My bonny bonny Thurstonland – I canny leave thee.' Whereupon he picked up his bags, walked back to the village, and stayed there till the day he died.

It was perhaps a wish to revive something of this old spirit of loyalty to the place which spurred various people to found a Community Association in the spring of 1975. The inaugural meeting was held one evening in the Village Hall – which was actually a cottage so named, and used by the Play Group, the Brownies and sometimes by other societies. I went along, this being one of the first occasions when I had done anything to make myself feel a part of Thurstonland – a curious omission, as I had already been living there for four years. Rather to my surprise I was elected on to the committee, which enabled me to gain a far fuller feeling of belonging to the village. The aims of the Association were 'to make a constructive contribution to the life of the community, and to protect its interests'. We were also anxious to establish contact with all the local societies. Considering the size of Thurstonland (about three hundred inhabitants), it was remarkable to discover that there were no fewer than thirteen such bodies. Alongside the ones you would expect, such as Scouts, Guides and the Cricket Club, there were some surprises – particularly the Druids. To my disappointment I discovered that these individuals no longer worshipped in groves wearing nothing but woad. They were in fact a small group of very respectable gentlemen who constituted a branch of the United Order of Druids, which was basically a Friendly Society. The Society itself had been founded in London in 1781, and the Thurstonland branch (officially Prince Albert Lodge no. 387) as long ago as 1851. Weekly contributions were made to help members who were sick or otherwise fallen on hard times. There was also a funeral grant that was paid on the death of a member, his wife, or even his second wife – but no provision was made for third or subsequent wives! It must have been a flourishing organisation in its heyday, since its centenary was celebrated with three busloads of members going on an outing to Skegness. Following a visit to a pub near Doncaster on the return journey, one bus lost its way, although it did eventually return to base. However, by 1975 the Druids had shrunk to a mere vestige of their former selves.

The new Community Association got off to a most successful start, leading to a mood of buoyancy and bonhomie among its members. During those first few years virtually everything we attempted came to fruition. We asked for an early morning bus – the bus duly appeared; for more flowers on the village green – they were blooming in less than no time. I was personally given the job of agitating for repairs to the seat on Baincliffe which commanded a magnificent view of the Holme Valley, and when one of my walks took me past the site and I saw that the old rotten plank had been replaced by a smart new one, I felt that after all I had not lived in vain. Discos, slide-shows and small concerts were organised; a new village notice-board went up; and the traditional Christmas Festival in the church was expanded into a momentous affair. Perhaps the crowning glory was the birth of the village's own newspaper, *The Thurstonland Thunderer*!

The *Thunderer* came out about once every two months. Occasionally its rumblings were preceded by a smaller effort called *The Lightning*, though I think its flashes were infrequent. There was at least one issue of *The Thurstonland Grumbler*, in which the editor complained about the apathy that had apparently descended on the inhabitants. But looking now at those early numbers, apathy seems the last thing in evidence. They absolutely sparkle with vitality and humour:

The annual general night out of the Football Club at the White Lion at Lockwood was highly successful – but details are lacking due to none of the participants being able to remember them.

Dear Sir,
   I would like to thank the person who burrowed through twelve-foot snowdrifts to get the *Thunderer* through to me. I could only catch a glimpse of this svelte mobile creature as he leapt gazelle-like across the snow. . . .

Even the adverts had a touch of humour: 'Wanted: home help. Must be fond of animals.' Presumably to cope with the four Rottweilers in the living room.

Thus the Community Association and its manifold activities flourished, until one evil day someone suggested that we get a better village hall. I do not know why it is, but somehow plans for buildings bring out the worst in people. (I was later to experience the same thing on an even grander scale with the Brontë Society, when an AGM almost turned into a riot.) But the strife in the Community Association was bad enough. Before we knew where we were there appeared plans A and B, and there might have been plans C, D, E and halfway to Z for all I can remember. Each plan attracted zealous advocates. Members of the Association who belonged to different factions, who would formerly have waved cheerily at one another from five fields' distance, now scarcely nodded as they passed in the village street. What all these plans entailed I can scarcely remember. The sad thing is that not only did we fail to get the big village hall, we even lost the tiny one we already had.

However, in those heady times of my first years in the village, these clouds hadn't started to gather. In retrospect (perhaps falsely) all seems light and happiness. Prominent among these recollections is the Annual Gala, which was held on the nearest Saturday to Midsummer's Day. The proceedings started at the Rose and Crown at 2.30 p.m. with a brass or silver band leading off the procession – which anyone could join in, fancy dress or not. There would be a pause at the war memorial for a rendition of 'Deep Harmony' and then it was on to the recreation ground. The first thing on arrival was the judging of the fancy dress. One local farmer used to turn up so convincingly disguised as an old woman that even his closest friends didn't recognise him. Then it was on with the main show, with Morris dancing, archery, comic football, a tug of war, trampolining, a ducking stool and much more.

I remember one year coming out of my house just as the Thurlstone Brass Band was passing the end of the avenue, making enough noise to wake the dead. The American lady who lived diagonally opposite came out at the same moment, and shouted to me across the road, 'Gee – what a lively little village this is!'

4

The Garden

'God Almighty first planted a garden. And indeed it is the purest of human pleasures.' I agree wholeheartedly with the opening words of Sir Francis Bacon's famous essay, but I cannot go along with his later remark that 'pools mar all, and make the garden unwholesome and full of flies and frogs'. In fact, as soon as I saw the house, with the area of quite virgin land around it, I decided at once to make a pond the centrepiece of the garden.

But there were other jobs to do beforehand. Drainage was a major problem, the house having been built on the gathering ground of a small stream called Town Moor Dike. The builder of this small estate had had quite a lot of problems with this, and was reputed to have gone bankrupt trying to combat them.

My front garden was on a slope and drained itself, but at the back I had to dig a 6ft-deep sump, and fill it with rubble. Three pipe and rubble drains ran into it. The little boy who lived in the house adjoining the bottom of the garden, who was then aged about 4, watched my activity with interest. When I had put all the earth back in the trenches he asked: 'Are you going to dig it up again sometime, to make sure those pipes are still there?' Surely an interesting example of early awareness of philosophical questions!

Once the drainage was finished I dug out the central pond, some 4ft by 8ft, and 18in deep, with a shallow shelf around the edge for marginal plants. I stocked the pond with two fan-tailed goldfish, two golden orfe and some water-snails, but of course other creatures soon moved in, such as water-boatmen, mosquito larvae, frogs and toads, the latter particularly liking the area where the pond could overflow, the water running through a patch of loose stones to join up with the pipes.

In digging out the pond I inevitably created high banks of loose earth. However, this was no problem as they provided an ideal position for my favourite plants: heathers. During the late summer and early autumn these glorious plants, both the common ling and the somewhat less common bell heather and cross-leaved heather, spread their purple glow over favoured areas of the Pennine moorland.

In a garden one can only hint at the scenery of such a place as Harbour Hill near Haworth, but even a hint is worthwhile. In general heathers are best planted in clumps of one variety contrasting with neighbouring clumps of other varieties, thereby providing diversity in both flowers and foliage, the foliage being especially important, since that is with you all the year round. Dotted around I placed dwarf conifers. However, I eventually found there were snags to these, especially as a lot of so-called dwarfs are really just slow growing, and given enough time will become quite large.

To shield the bare bricks at the back of the house I planted clematis, beneath which were sink gardens, and at the bottom some pussy willow beyond my neighbour's fence provided a partial screen. Along both sides I had specimen shrubs: snowberry, firethorn (pyracantha), climbing hydrangea, berberis Darwinia and mock-orange. The rest of the garden was put down to lawn, with one side curving to embrace the central pond. I also created a smaller pond closer to the house.

I tended to work in the garden in fits and starts. Having a full-time job meant I couldn't devote as much time to it as I might wish. Then there were other interruptions – mainly girls. For weeks or months the weeds would flourish undisturbed, no doubt wondering at their good fortune. Then suddenly I would return to the attack, and vent my spleen against womankind on the helpless twitch grass and shepherd's purse, not to mention any cultivars that had got out of hand. And for a while the place would be immaculate again – until the cycle repeated itself.

Work on a garden may be a pleasure in itself, but it is important to spend some time there simply doing nothing. The modern world, with all its subtle pressures, discourages doing nothing – but occasionally I have found a space for this activity (or inactivity). I remember once at Altea in Spain spending two hours on the deserted beach just watching the sun setting. On another occasion I devoted a similar span of time to observing the tide coming in at Bowness-on-Solway. In both instances I found the experience rewarding, and felt the time had been well spent.

My favourite spot for doing nothing was the edge of the lawn nearest the fishpond. Here one could spread out a groundsheet on sunny days, and observe the pond-life: the golden orfe basking on the surface, or dashing furiously around the sides; the water-boatmen congregated in a great mass, which looked like a rugby scrum; the swarms of tadpoles wriggling in clusters at the water's edge; and the frogs making love – apparently with no thought for privacy.

The garden was also a useful place for observing humankind, particularly the playing and quarrelling of children. I recollect once watching a girl of about 7 walloping her younger sister, and accompanying the action with the words 'what big sisters say, big sisters mean'. On another occasion there was a tent pitched on the next-door neighbour's lawn, and various small boys and girls were bickering around it. I knew one of the boys, a lad named Paul, and asked him what was going on:

Paul: 'We're playing at happy families.'
Self: 'There's an awful lot of quarrelling going on.'
Paul: 'Well, you've got to be realistic you know.'

While apparently absorbed in the weeding, I would listen to the children playing rhyming games, memorise them and record them in a notebook. Here are two examples:

Please miss
My mother miss
She told me miss
To tell you miss
That I miss
Won't miss
Be at school
Tomorrow miss.

D'you want a cigarette sir
No sir
Why sir?
Because I've got a cold sir
Where d'you get the cold sir?
Up the North Pole sir
Catching polar bears sir
How many did you catch sir?
None sir
But they caught me sir.

This last was chanted by a small girl as she kept two tennis balls in the air, while bouncing them against a wall.

The children, like the flowers, seemed to emerge in the spring. In fact during the winter months one might have assumed that all Thurstonland was hibernating. Only the rhythmic thumping as my neighbour played his favourite Cat Stevens record extra loudly reminded me that there were other dwellers above ground.

Then, perhaps on a mild day in March, things would suddenly come to life. Diligent gardeners emerged clutching secateurs, to prune the roses or the clematis. In my own garden the winter-flowering jasmine would still be yellow, while among the heathers erica darleyensis and silberschmelze were in bloom. In the pond the water trollius started showing colour, and at the same time great dollops of frog-spawn appeared; the full stops at the centre eventually turned to commas before the tadpoles emerged, until the edges of the pond became a mass of black wriggling bodies. They seemed to like to be as close to the edge as possible, and even crammed themselves into the overflows of water in the chinks of the crazy-paving surround.

April, and the chionodoxas and scilla sibiricas display their exquisite blue flowers. The pussy willow at the bottom is in bloom, and the blue-tits are raising a brood in the nesting-box. On 29 May 1978 I observed in my gardening notes: 'With the late winter and the abrupt start of summer, we virtually didn't have a spring this year.' Some years it would seem like that. Even in late spring one might see the distant Pennines coated with snow, at least in the early morning. And then suddenly it

Nature's egalitarian revolution . . . a universal whiteness. (Author's collection)

would be sweltering: ladybirds appearing everywhere, goldfish lazing near the pond's surface, and midges, dragonflies and mayflies dancing above it. But of course this abruptness is an illusion. Nature pursues its secret gradual changes but man, always in a hurry, fails to notice them.

When summer truly comes then is the time to be lazy. The traditional chores for this time of the year are lawn mowing and hedge trimming. But once these are out of the way, we must select our favourite garden spot, and then read a book, listen to the radio (with the sound turned down low so as not to annoy the neighbours) or simply do nothing. By then the pieris formosa Forrestii will be showing off both its lily-of-the-valley-like flowers and its bright red bracts, and the hanging baskets will be at their most jingoistic, with the red of geranium, the white of alyssum and the blue of lobelia. Against the house wall the purple clematis Jackmanii is in full bloom. At its best this is a superb sight. The finest specimen I ever saw was at Wylam on the Tyne, growing on a south-facing cottage wall, looking towards a stretch of land where George Stephenson first experimented with steam locomotion.

By mid-July the tadpoles are just entering froghood. In the final stages of metamorphosis their bodies appear to shrink – fairly large tadpoles become very little frogs, which look especially strange when they already have frogs' bodies, but still have their long tadpole tails.

Autumn was always heralded by a great twittering of sparrows in the nearby trees, the swallows starting to gather together and the water-boatmen forming exceptionally large rugby scrums. And the garden had a particular beauty in September, especially with the late afternoon sunlight glinting on the soft russet foliage of 'Golden Drop' (a cultivated bell heather) and on the feathery strands of the water reeds. Elsewhere on the heather banks all the lings and the Cornish heathers would be in bloom, while the honeysuckle was covered in pale orange berries and a few flowers still clung bravely to the mimulus.

One interesting feature of autumn is the occasional appearance of 'lammas shoots' on plants that normally bloom much earlier in the year. Some of these buds don't make it into flowers, but when the daylight length returns to that of their usual time of flowering, these odd stragglers suddenly bloom. There is something rather pathetic about these last fruitless attempts at procreation, especially if the insects that pollinate them are no longer around.

Neither in the garden nor elsewhere is winter an entirely colourless season. In late autumn the winter-flowering jasmine against the front wall starts to show yellow, and continues right into the spring. Among the heathers 'Winter Beauty' always lives up to its name, and the Daphne Mezereum in a neighbour's plot provides another welcome splash of colour. A nearby beech hedge often retains its autumn tints right through until the spring. But a time much loved by some (especially children and lazy gardeners) was when snow covered everything. Thus, in nature's own egalitarian revolution, the plots of the most active horticulturalists and those of the idle and ignorant alike assumed a universal whiteness.

5

Walks

Going for a walk must be one of our great enduring pleasures, and there has scarcely been a day of my life when I haven't indulged in it. Even when working in big cities I have often gone 'once round the block' in the lunch hour, and seen something in nature or human life to amuse me: the changing state of the trees by the roadside; the boisterous riot of a school playground. Of course, living in a small village one is highly privileged. A mere five minutes and you are away from houses, so that no walk is too short to be worth doing. The stroll in the early summer morning before anyone else is up, watching the dawn lighting the sky, the white mist clearing, the odd hare hurrying away from the path; or the amble in the evening after the fret of a day's work, seeing the last rays of sunlight shining on the whites of the cricketers, on the bands of new-mown hay, on the fireweed standing up against the darkening sky – all these refresh the soul, relieving the stress.

One obvious dilemma with walks is the question of companionship. At a certain stage I joined a rambling club. This was fine socially, and friendships were formed which persist till this day. But from the point of view of the walk itself – the scenes, the sense of nature – much was lost. It was all experienced through a blur of conversation. Eventually I felt there was more loss than gain, and let my membership lapse. Small groups are not much better – in fact the old saying 'two's company, but three's a crowd' holds a great deal of truth. Thus the ideal is probably one trusted companion, preferably someone with a similar walking speed and congenial interests (those who would walk into the sunset discussing income tax are best avoided). The sex of the companion is almost irrelevant – one ex-girlfriend became a splendid fellow walker, once she had learnt to slacken her pace a bit. Of my male friends I might especially mention Ken (the dedicatee of this book), and Simon, whose minute knowledge of plants and animals makes a walk with him something of an education, as well as a pleasure.

The companion of course doesn't have to be human – there are also dogs. The praise of dogs as friends is of course an old theme. Sir Walter Scott nearly always wrote with his favourite dog at his feet, and Emily Brontë's preference for dogs over humans was proverbial. When it comes to company on walks they have many virtues: they never bore you with stupid conversation, yet they provide the comfort of a loyal friend close by. However, while humans appreciate nature primarily through their eyes, canines enjoy it primarily via their nostrils – and this can lead to a certain irritation. Up on the high moors, where bitch urine is a rare commodity, one's dog will trot along for hours without deviating. But then on the home stretch at last, when the walker begins to yearn for the awaiting cup of tea, the dog suddenly begins dashing up to trees and lampposts as if the walk were just commencing.

The final possibility, and one that is certainly not to be despised, is walking alone. If the mood is right this can be most enjoyable; there is no one to distract you, or demand to go a different way. And you can rest at will, and let the sights, sounds and smells around you seep into your being. Curiously enough, while walking alone one seldom feels lonely.

Sometimes quite short walks lead to some minor adventure or unexplained mystery. I recollect once walking to Farnley Tyas and noticing in a nearby field something which looked like a gigantic dog-basket, alongside a very large piece of blue material. I was insufficiently curious to investigate at the time, and only learnt the explanation later. The story seemed like some strange echo of the village's Scandinavian origin. It had all started at six that morning, when a Norwegian gentleman named Thor Carlton set off in his hot-air balloon from Norwich, intending to fly to Oslo. Alas, contrary winds drove him from his intended course, and he ended up crash-landing ignominiously at Thurstonland; apparently, he smashed through some electric cables, collided with a dry-stone wall and was dragged across a field before ending up on top of another wall – a sequence of events which Thor apparently described as 'normal'. Fortunately the Beaumont family came to his rescue, providing him with the comforts of a cup of tea, a somewhat late siesta, a meal and a bed for the night – thus proving that the tradition of hospitality to strangers is by no means lost.

There was plenty of interest without going for more than a mile or two from Thurstonland: the deserted village in the wood near Woodsome Lees, with the crumbling ruins where once the stream had turned a millwheel; the beautiful small valley of Ellen Springs, always covered in bluebells in April; and the summit of Pike Stye, with its wonderful view across the Holme Valley to the Pennines. Further afield there were many fine valley walks, as well as rambles on the tops – 'moor bashing' as the local walking fraternity called it. Unfortunately there didn't seem to be many routes that combined the two, as the lower slopes of the moors were often private land. One exception was a walk which started at Digley Reservoir, crossed the dam between it and Bilberry Reservoir (the bursting of which caused the famous Holmfirth flood of 1852), and followed a track to Godbent Lodge, and thence to the curiously named Blackpool Bridge. From here you could make your own route, perhaps to the very high Marsden Wood (these small elevated woods are a feature of some parts of the Pennines; there is another example just above Shedden Clough near Todmorden), or to the waterfall in Issues Clough, or perhaps wander on the plateau of Black Hill – but this is an unpleasant place in misty conditions.

When it comes to slightly more ambitious ventures, the area to the east is largely industrial and scarcely walker's country, while to the west are the high bleak Pennine

The Yorkshire Dales, bracing and invigorating. Here are the heather moors between Kettlewell and Litton. (Author's collection)

Moors. To the south lie the Peak District and the Derbyshire Dales, which are very beautiful no doubt and full of interest – yet I find them strangely melancholy. Far more to my liking is the area to the north: the Yorkshire Dales – Arkengarthdale, Swaledale, Wensleydale, Nidderdale, Wharfedale and Airedale. Those are perhaps the best known, but there are numerous lesser dales, not to mention Calderdale, which is too built-up to be added to the scenic six but which has a strong fascination all of its own. There is something bracing and invigorating about the Dales, something that makes one grateful for the gift of life. And the scenery is so varied: the ancient limestone cliffs of Malham, the strange potholes around Ingleborough, the churning dark waterfall at West Burton, alternating darkness and light.

Among my many walks in the Yorkshire Dales, a three-day excursion in the exceptionally hot summer of 1976 remains especially clear in my memory – mainly the final stretch, coming down the slopes of Great Whernside on a warm August afternoon to the Youth Hostel at Kettlewell. The next day I tried to capture the experience in a poem called Homeward to Kettlewell. It is written in a style which I no longer pursue, but I print it below without change, since nothing I could write now would capture the feeling so vividly:

Homeward to Kettlewell –
Westward and straight to the rays of the yellow sun,
Sinking and slipping
On the sweeping curve of the hillside's spur,
Where the grassy path is broad and dry and soft,
And the mind is a wilting dusk of weariness.

Down there in Kettlewell
There will be food and drink,
Hot water to wash in,
And clean, clean sheets
Waiting for daylight's end.
There in the common room
I can sink in the soft embrace of an easy chair,
Write up my notes of the day's events,
And chew the cud of its wayward memories:
Of the curious peat hag
That looked like a witch's cottage
All thatched with bilberries;
Of the kestrel unaware
Resting with folded wings near where I stood;
Of the scarlet tips of the lichen;
Of the tiny antlers of the reindeer moss;
Of the soft trailing lace of the crowberry;
And the frightened skylark's sudden flight,
And the grouse's hostile cry:
'Go back, go back, go back'.

Down now to Kettlewell –
Down past the last small farm,
Over a wall,
Open and close the final gate,
Placing the hook in the staple –
Yes – that's right.
Sheep on the uprake bleating,
Cows on the fossil mud
Staring and mooing
Down past the camp and the caravans –
Two young girls sit in the sun reading their comics,

Two lovers are on the bed
Just glimpsed through the tent flap
He lying over her
Kissing and petting
(Seems a bit early for that).
Down by the stream
A little boy has been bathing,
Now he stands wrapped in his orange towel;
The farmer's wife
Carries two pails of milk along the lane;
The cat at the post office
Paws playfully at a dead robin;
A dog is about to bark,
But decides not to bother
(After all it's only another bloody rambler);
And the phlox in the gardens
Are vivid magenta against the purple clematis.

We turn into a side road,
And there is the hostel
Redolent with the smell of sweaty socks
And bangers and beans and foot ointment;
The girls in the common room are giggling,
And someone is playing Beethoven on the piano,
But soon that is drowned
As an avalanche of noisy kids descends the stairs,
And the supper bell rings out its clarion.

6

The Pennine Way

Moving from one place to another is a strange sensation and sometimes difficult to accept. John Clare, when he had shifted no more than 4 miles from Helpstone to Northborough, lamented the change through many verses in his poem 'The Flitting', even fearing that the well-springs of his poetic inspiration would be dried up by the move. I know how he felt. Although actually born in Sussex, I had moved around quite a bit. The move to Yorkshire wasn't from the south but from the north – from Northumberland. The six years I spent there held some painful memories, especially a broken marriage. But inevitably there were also times of great happiness, and however much I liked my new Yorkshire surroundings a certain yearning remained. One possible therapy for this state of mind (not one I have read of, merely experienced) is to walk from the one place to the other; no amount of travelling by other means has the same effect. The fact that one's own two feet can carry you there is somehow reassuring, and the former discord becomes a harmony.

When it came to walking from my part of Yorkshire to Northumberland there was an obvious route to follow – the Pennine Way – even if it did somewhat over-do the job by starting in Derbyshire and carrying on to Scotland.

The Pennine Way is one of the longest footpaths in Britain, stretching 270 miles from Edale in Derbyshire to Kirk Yetholm, just over the Scottish border. It was the idea of Tom Stephenson, one-time secretary of the Ramblers' Association, who worked for over thirty years to bring the concept to fruition. The complete footpath was officially opened on 24 April 1965, with a gathering by the side of Malham Tarn.

The name 'Pennine Way' is something of a misnomer, in that the route embraces quite a bit more than the Pennines. Starting at the south end the first 15 miles or so takes you through the Peak District, while at the northern end two days are spent crossing the valley of the Tyne, and two more negotiating the Cheviots. To describe it as a footpath is also misleading – in places it is no more than a number of widely separated markers across pathless moorland. And far from sticking to the Pennine watershed, it meanders up the middle of northern England, managing to pass en route a remarkable number of places with divergent interests: literary (Top Withens, Dotheboys Hall), geological (Malham Cove) and historical (Hadrian's Wall). The walker encounters four of the finest English waterfalls (Hardraw Force,

High Force, Cauldron Snout and Hareshaw Linn) and crosses a wide variety of terrain: moorlands, arable land, forests and river valleys. Oddly enough, at two points the route leads straight through somebody's garden!

It was on 23 May 1975 that I went by train to Edale in Derbyshire, for the start of something which, to a man of my mundane lifestyle, was quite an adventure. From the outside Edale Hostel was ablaze with rhododendron flowers; inside it was a riot of noisy kids. After booking in and eating the evening meal, I made my escape to the nearby hamlet of Grindsbrook Booth, where I had a drink at the Nags Head in the company of two young men called Malcolm and Graham, whose similarly hooked noses indicated they were brothers. As I walked back, the little white tails of rabbits scurried around in the darkness by the stream side. A full moon was slowly rising above Back Tor, and in the west the faint glow where the sun had set showed up beyond the black outline of Kinder Scout.

At the hostel I met three men who were to cross my path several times in the next seventeen days. Andrew was about 40 and was blessed with balding lank hair and a rather blunt Lancashire way of putting things; his friend Charlie was 58 and had an expression of quiet amusement permanently set on his sunburnt face. The third man was a middle-aged schoolmaster named Neville Janes.

The next morning Andrew and Charlie set off early. Neville intended to start the Pennine Way on the following day, and to devote today to a wander over Kinder Scout. It was in Neville's company that I set off. The day was cold and cloudy, with a keen wind blowing. As we walked up the valley of Grindsbrook a cuckoo was singing somewhere in the woods to our left. The lower hillsides were vivid green with the newly leafing bilberries, their tiny pink flowers being quite inconspicuous. We clambered up a boulder and scree-filled gully, and arrived on the great undulating boggy plateau of Kinder Scout. This was familiar country to me, and I had no excuse for going astray. Nevertheless I made the classic mistake of just following the person in front – who happened to be a Polish lady who wasn't intending to follow the Pennine Way. We talked to her for a while, and after she left us I realised we were lost – and the top of Kinder Scout is a most deceptive place, even to those familiar with it. We floundered on through various bogs, and I think Neville feared he was going to sink forever. However, our floundering brought us eventually to the highest point, at 2,088ft. A small party was up there already. We asked if they were walking the Pennine Way, but it turned out they were hiking over to the Snake Inn for a drink.

We contemplated going with them, but instead muddled on, and eventually the Mermaid's Pool and the tumbled rocks of Kinder Downfall came into view. A bit further on I parted from Neville (although not forever, as it turned out), and after a while sat down to lunch. I was hungry, and felt much satisfaction in setting out the hostel's packed lunch and pouring my tea. I had no sooner done so, however, than a ram charged towards me, seized my roll and knocked the tea all over my erstwhile clean towel. Although normally kind to animals, I was so angry that I picked up my rucksack and belted it.

Having finished what remained of my lunch, I walked to the north-west corner of Kinder Scout, and down into a dip and on to Mill Hill, where I met a couple of

'The Kiss', Bleaklow – the only bit of sex on the Pennine Way, according to Alfred Wainwright.
(Author's collection)

young men, one of them wearing a deer-stalker. They appeared to be climbing up from Hayfield, and I assumed they weren't walking the Pennine Way. Later I learnt that they were thoroughly lost, and too ashamed of themselves to ask the way. We only exchanged a few words at the time, but I was to see more of them later. Their names were Eric and Edmund.

The next summit is Bleaklow – a great sprawling mass of bog that is definitely bleak, if not particularly low. The one spot likely to cheer the love-lorn wanderer is 'The Kiss' (officially the Wain Stones), two rocks that, seen from a certain angle, resemble a couple kissing. Wainwright* calls it the only bit of sex on the Pennine Way – but this surely depends on the individual.

It had been a tiring day, and it was good to slacken my pace as I descended Bleaklow and walked round Torside Reservoir to Crowden Hostel. The sun was now shining brilliantly on the beautiful trunks of the silver birches by the roadside. At the hostel I met two more unforgettable characters: John and Arthur. They were chatting away in the dormitory so heartily that I assumed they were lifelong friends. In fact they had only just met. John was 48, a foundry worker from Chorley in Lancashire (where the Chorley cakes come from). He was a short-distance runner and looked

* Alfred Wainwright, *Pennine Way Companion*, Westmorland Gazette, 1968.

extremely fit. He had had little experience of walking, but was doing the Pennine Way as a sponsored venture in aid of an extension to the local Sunday School. At each halt one of the church dignitaries would meet him with a bar of chocolate and a clean pair of underpants! Arthur was a middle-aged bachelor from Accrington. He had done some stretches of the route so often that, according to the wife of the warden at Mankinholes, the cairns nodded to him as he went past! He was also one of the kindest people I have ever met, constantly doing people good turns, even when they didn't want them. (I remember him giving a lady directions for the Pennine Way, only to be told that she was going to the nearby village shop for some butter.) These two men had one thing in common – a tremendous sense of humour. Also at the hostel that evening were Eric and Edmund, who had finally got back on track.

To describe each day in the same detail as the first would turn this chapter into a book, so vivid are my memories from those seventeen days. There are of course the landscapes, but there are also the portraits; some people that I met for only a few hours seemed to assume a major importance in my life story. And then there were the trivialities (very important at the time), such as what one ate (I remember vast quantities of Kendal Mint Cake) and how one coped with sore feet (stuffing raw sheep's wool into your boots can be recommended).

The second day I walked with Eric and Edmund. I was glad of their company for it was little more than a 25-mile squelch through peat hags, while the weather was one long misery of drizzling rain. One moment of respite and nostalgia came when I caught a very distant view of Thurstonland – the two low hills and the tiny jab of the church steeple on the saddle between them. By early evening we had passed Warland Reservoir, and here I parted from my companions and descended the hillside to Mankinholes Hostel. I was so tired I had to force myself to clamber over the tussock grass on that last steep slope. The sun had finally come out, and over everything there was a warm glow of evening light: it shone on the rough slopes below Stoodley Pike and lit the square tower of Heptonstall Church on the wooded hill beyond. Down in the Calder Valley below me the fields were a vivid green, and in the middle ground the curious Lumbutts water tower was reflected in the stagnant mill pond.

That evening at Mankinholes proved something of a foretaste of things to come. A lecture and slide-show on local architecture was given by an antiquarian of small stature and very characteristic mannerisms. Afterwards I went to the pub, then called the Dog and Partridge but since renamed the Top Brink. Here I fell in with three very young lads from Suffolk who called themselves the 'Three Musketeers'. They had set themselves the almost impossible task (for them) of doing the Pennine Way in ten days. I later discovered that their idea of 'doing' it included hopping on a bus whenever they were tired. One thing bound them together apart from walking – they were all 'girl mad' (not that I claim to be totally indifferent to them) and the evening turned into one long session of ogling the local beauties. Feeling eventually that I was marginally too old for this activity, I retired to the hostel.

*Ken (left) and Charlie
near Stoodley Pike.*
(Author's collection)

The next day was the longest stretch – at least as I did it, covering 28 miles to Earby. Eight of us set off northwards from Mankinholes. The first mishap occurred a few hundred yards from the hostel, when Charlie suddenly realised he'd forgotten his rubber-knobbed stick, of which he was inordinately fond. Arthur immediately dashed back for it. Arthur continued to guide and shepherd us for the rest of the day. As we passed Top Withens he had the kindness to inform us that 'It's in that book what those Brontë people wrote about like.'

Next day we again had Arthur to direct us, but only as far as the Leeds–Liverpool Canal, where he shook hands with us all and then set off westwards. He had been so helpful that we were rather lost without him, and were forced once more to stick our noses into the pages of Wainwright.

The Pennine Way is full of contrasts, and after those first three days of predominantly bleak moorland, we were now walking through lush meadows and verdant valleys. I especially remember the scene as we entered Gargrave: before us stood the church and the stone-built houses set among the deep green trees; around us were fertile fields with cows and sheep contentedly grazing; overhead rooks were cawing and lapwings crying; and everything was filled with a sense of noon and early summer. The last part of that day saw us on a fine stretch of path following the white-pebbled banks of the Aire up to the limestone cliffs of Malham. We met up with a father and son who were keen ornithologists – Mick and Dad as we called them. Mick had a very mobile face which lit up with a sudden expression of joy whenever he saw a bird of interest, while Dad's countenance bore signs of an enviable state of continuous contentment.

'Look, Dad, look – a dipper,' Mick shouted excitedly, 'over there where the wall juts into the stream.'

Father and son duly scrutinised it through binoculars, which they then passed to me. I was delighted with the clear view of this great haunter of the upland streams. But there were plenty of other birds to interest them: curlews, with their plaintive cry and long curved bills, flew across the fields; sand martins darted around the river banks; and redshanks flashed past quite close to us.

It is always exciting to see in reality something which one has known from pictures since childhood. Thus it was as we walked up the final green stretch of the Aire, and saw Malham before us. In the middle-ground was the village, and beyond it the great limestone sweep of Malham Cove – 300ft of banded rock layers, with a pattern like a viaduct in the centre, where an ancient waterfall had once crashed over

Janet. (Author's collection)

Janet's Foss near Malham. (Author's collection)

the face, before the stream went underground. I had another reason for being excited. Here I was meeting Janet Mear, an attractive 20-year-old nurse, with whom I had had a very brief romance, followed by a friendship which remains to this day. After a shower and a meal at the hostel I went back out into the fresh evening air. Janet was waiting for me on a seat by the post office, and together we set off along the lane towards Gordale Scar. At Janet's Foss she had a fancy to be photographed beside her namesake waterfall. Then we recrossed the narrow lane, and walked towards the scar.

Gordale reveals its splendours gradually, like a shy girl making love. We traversed the green meadow scattered over with tents as the dusk was coming on. The Gordale Beck gurgled down its pebbled course, and the high limestone cliffs brooded above, their ledges dotted with dark stunted yews. Around a wonderful twist in the path suddenly the full chasm appeared, with the lower waterfall tumbling over tufa rocks which have the look of well-weathered driftwood. We clambered up

Gordale, with the two waterfalls.
(Author's collection)

the slippery rocks to the right of the fall, and from there could see the higher fall pouring out of a natural window. Some more scrambling and we were at the top.

We explored the area above the gorge, and for a short while were out of sight of each other. When I turned to look for her, Janet had vanished. I assumed she had gone higher up the stream, and followed in that direction. There was no sign of her.

'Janet,' I called, alarmed.

There was no answer. I wondered for a moment if she had fallen over the waterfall, and peered down from the rocks above, but there were no ghastly remains splattered below. I began to think she was just an apparition, capable of instant disappearance. Eventually I found her quite unconcerned at the bottom of the gorge. She had just wandered off.

Janet pitched her tent that night not in the approved camping site but surreptitiously in a field down by the Aire. By the time we had erected the tent it was 10.20 p.m. The hostel closed at 10.30 p.m. – I would have to hurry back. There was just enough light for me to make out the form of a fleeting hare scurrying through the darkness as I walked quickly along the riverside fields. Venus was glowing in the west, and the curlews were crying out their melancholy rising call.

The next day was one long haul over Fountains Fell and Pen-y-ghent to Horton-in-Ribblesdale. Here we all went into the Pen-y-ghent café and ordered Chorley cakes. These products of John's home town had been the subject of many jokes along the way, with someone insisting that they were really only Eccles cakes that had been squashed with a mallet!

That night there was a sharp frost and the next morning the sun rose up in a clear sky, and soon it was warm, with only a few streamers of mist slithering down the stepped profile of Pen-y-ghent. Before our departure I remember a fleeting glimpse of John setting forth with resolute step, like Christian journeying to the Eternal City. That was the last I saw of him. Despite the bright start the weather soon became so cold and misty that we saw no scenery worth mentioning. My clearest recollection is of the conversation, especially with Mick, whom I found a fascinating person, both extremely practical yet somehow set apart from the mundane run of this world.

Janet's two days of walking with me ended at Hawes. A quick kiss and she was on the bus to Ripon. Next day we followed the route from Hawes to Keld, over the big bleak hump of Great Shunner Fell. On its summit Andrew composed a variation on a well-known epigram:

> I do not like thee Shunner Fell,
> The reason why I cannot tell,
> But this I know and know full well,
> I do not like thee Shunner Fell.

The descent was more pleasant, offering a few glimpses of Upper Swaledale, as well as a distant view to the north-west of the hills around Cross Fell, the highest of the Pennines. Further to the west could be seen the outlines of the Lake District. As we approached the delightful village of Thwaite we fell in with a local doctor who invited us all round to his cottage for refreshments. It was a beautiful place, with very thick stone walls. On the mantelpiece I remember there was a hatter's iron, popularly known as a 'weasel'. (The apparently nonsensical line 'pop goes the weasel' seemingly refers to a hatter being so extravagant that he is forced to pawn the tools of his trade.) There was also an igloo oven – that is, a very small oven designed to make use of the hot ash from the fire, and having a loose brick to give an opening to the main chimney flue.

The stretch from Thwaite to Keld is possibly the most beautiful of the whole Pennine Way. The valley of the Swale beneath us was glowing in the warmth of afternoon sunlight, the grassy slopes dotted with small stunted hawthorns. In the side valley of Swinner Gill a stream could be seen descending in white cascades, and the Swale itself rippled over innumerable small falls. Bird cherries were in white blossom nearby, and many wild flowers grew beside the footpath. Above great cumulus clouds moved majestically across the turquoise sky.

Of Keld itself I remember mainly the waterfalls and the towering limestone cliffs. The hostel, too, was memorable. As we went in through the door we saw a card pinned to the notice-board. It read 'We made it!' and was signed 'The Three Musketeers'. I keep it yet as a souvenir.

After the meal I knocked on the door of the staff kitchen and asked for a chore. My knock was answered by a most delightful young cook, a pretty girl in a very old-fashioned sort of way, like something out of 'Merrie England'. Beyond her a great jollification was in progress. She gave me the job of assembling the crockery ready for tomorrow's breakfasts, and between bursts of hilarity offered an explanation:

'Oh, but you must forgive me tonight. I've just got engaged. Here, see.'
'Congratulations.'
'Yes – and we're all in the midst of a party. I'm so busy I haven't had time to open me presents.'

A young couple named Linda and John joined me at Keld, and walked with me for most of the following day. (Charlie, Andrew and the others had their separate plans, and I didn't see them again.) The terrain for that day was somewhat monotonous. The only highlights were a drink at Tan Hill (the highest pub in England) and my sinking in a bog up to my thighs. Parting from Linda and John at Sleightholme Farm really marked the end of the first half of the Pennine Way as I experienced it. Hitherto I had had company nearly all the time, but thereafter I was predominantly on my own. I have always felt that congenial company is the greatest of all pleasures, but if I am honest it must be admitted that I enjoyed the second half of the journey more than the first.

Bereft of the distractions of society, nature became something to be experienced at a much deeper level: the changing cloud-patterns; the wild flowers; the songs of the birds. In addition to the people and the landscape, the second half was also remarkable for the weather. The English weather is notoriously changeable, but it can be changeable in a rather tedious way, with wet days following dry days, thereby providing the bare elements for polite conversation. But that June it became totally eccentric. The sharp frost at Horton-in-Ribblesdale proved to be a warning of things to come.

Four days later I was just leaving my night's accommodation at Middleton-in-Teesdale when my landlady said: 'Sorry to tell you, but it's started snowing.' This was on 2 June! That day I was doing the short but beautiful stretch up the Tees Valley to Langdon Beck Hostel. The snow soon turned to sleet, and thereafter spells of sunshine alternated with sleet and snow. As I walked on my body warmed up, and I could appreciate the scenery. On one side the brown peat-stained waters of the River Tees dashed over black dolerite rocks, with innumerable cascades and small islands in mid-stream. The banks were full of wild flowers, some of them rare. There was a sort of wild denticulata, and various members of the buttercup family. The hills above the valley were white with the morning's snow.

En route I passed the two famous waterfalls, Low Force and High Force. At the former I was overtaken by about fifteen soldiers, all members of the Royal Signals (my own regiment when I did National Service). It was curious to think that they

Low Force, Teesdale. (Author's collection)

were walking the Pennine Way as a toughening-up exercise, while I was doing it for pleasure. At High Force I had lunch in the company of their two sergeants, who were acting as 'sweepers'. One of them came from Golcar just outside Huddersfield.

As I approached Langdon Beck Hostel the weather deteriorated, and soon after my arrival a full-blown snowstorm was raging outside, with large flakes rushing past the window and settling everywhere. Someone suggested we should sing Christmas carols! I was drinking tea in the common room with a geology student named Desmond when a Mr Wyndham from Stanhope came in and asked: 'Have you two seen Neville Janes?' This was the name of the retired schoolmaster from whom I had parted on the top of Kinder Scout many days before. Desmond, however, had apparently seen him earlier that day.

Having left a message for him, Mr Wyndham departed. We learnt later that after leaving the hostel he met some character in a snow-covered cagoule coming towards him:

'Excuse me – but have you seen my friend Neville Janes?'
'I am Neville Janes,' came the answer.

I was excited that evening. The next day we would be walking up the last stretches of Teesdale, over the main Pennine watershed, and down via High Cup to the Eden Valley. It is one of the best days of the Pennine Way in any case, but in the present weather conditions it promised to be something of an adventure. Overnight, however, the snow changed to rain, and by morning only the higher hills retained it.

Cauldron Snout, Teesdale. (Author's collection)

Snow on Cross Fell. (Author's collection)

It was therefore somewhat less of a challenge, but none the less highly enjoyable, as Desmond and I tramped up beside the Tees, beneath the crags of Falcon Clints, around the base of the foaming waters of Cauldron Snout, and up by the Maize Beck to the low limestone cliffs of Maizebeck Scar. From there the route lay over a stretch of relatively flat ground, which marks the main English watershed. Then we got our first glimpse of High Cup, the most spectacular scene on the whole Pennine Way. It suddenly appeared beneath us, a great symmetrical U-shape that looked as if it had been scooped out of the hills by a giant with a rounded chisel. Around its upper edge the vertical columns of the Whin Sill stood like rows of organ pipes, and from the moors above numerous becks cascaded down, tumbling over the rocks in long thin waterfalls, to join together in a meandering river far below. And beyond this stretched the Valley of the Eden, with woods and fields, some red with freshly ploughed earth, some green, some yellow, and above the wide pastoral valley loomed the Lake District mountains, their summits edged with snow, and a thin veil of rain falling from the dark clouds overhead.

The June winter still hadn't given up. Next day we were having lunch on the summit of Cross Fell in the company of our army friends (we had crossed and recrossed paths many times). I suppose being bombarded with hailstones on 4 June would have been enough to make St Francis of Assisi mutter a mild curse. The British Army has of course never been noted for its restraint in this respect, and the expletives were almost as numerous as the hailstones. But that really was the mini-winter's final fling. As Desmond and I descended the eastern slopes, past the old lead mines and the spoil heaps littered with fluorspar, the sun was shining.

Two days later, as I emerged from the coolness of Wark Forest, the open countryside was bathed in warmth. I passed the beautiful old farmhouse of Low Stead, crossed some slight but shapely hills and climbed up to Shitlington Crags – a name that provokes the inevitable jokes in Wainwright. (Was there any connection with the John Storthes of Shittylington who features in the early history of Thurstonland, I wonder?) And then beyond the crags was a vast area of rough grazing land, full of cows and sheep. Writers often speak of the peace and quiet of the countryside, yet the countryside has its own times of hustle and bustle, and early evening seems to be one of them.

As I crossed that rough pasture, with the sun declining but still warm, the fields around me were full of activity. The cows mooed as they moved across the grassland, and a black bull in the distance was bellowing; lambs bleated and ran to their mothers; lapwings flew aggressively at me as I neared their nests; larks sang in the almost cloudless sky; moths fluttered among the rough grass; and gnats played out a frantic love-dance above the humid heat of the stagnant pools. This was nature's rush-hour – as lively as man's, but infinitely more beautiful.

Two days later and the warmth had turned into a heatwave as I crossed the Cheviots. In every direction there were great rounded summits, receding into a blue-grey haze. They all looked much alike, and it needed some careful reading of the map to work out what was what. Between Brownhart Law and Lamb Hill both the Pennine Way and the English/Scottish border follow a long bend to the north-east, roughly following the watershed. I decided to ignore the official route and strike straight across the Buckham Valley. I was pleased to find that the Buckham Wall's Burn was full of fish. Beyond this I crossed the slopes of Wedder Hill to Rennies Burn, and climbed upwards beside the tributary which descends from Lamb Hill. Here I found a beautiful pool into which fell a small waterfall. The banks were smooth and grassy, and the bottom sandy. It was irresistible. I stripped off and jumped into the cool water. Bliss! I had never felt so refreshed, and set off again like a resurrected spirit.

So much for the weather. What of the people? I lost sight of Neville Janes a few fields beyond Langdon Beck Hostel, and this time he was lost forever. Desmond I said goodbye to at Garrigill. From that last week of the walk there are two memories outstanding: Sheila Murray and Joe Hutton.

I met Sheila Murray at Byrness Hostel. As I ate my meal, she sat down at a nearby table, turned her chair towards me and started a conversation. She was in her late 20s, and at first glance had that healthy outdoor look which one associated with girl ramblers: red, sunburnt cheeks and greeny eyes. Unusually, however, her hair was already turning grey. Sheila talked about herself in a way that didn't seem at all immodest, and a strange tale emerged. She had in her earlier years run a pottery in Ireland and indeed was an authority on pottery and glassware, having had books published on both subjects. Then for some reason she had decided to emerge from this Celtic twilight world and step straight into the twentieth century. She became an

Rowhope Farm. (Author's collection)

air hostess. Meanwhile, it was discovered that she was suffering from some terrible disease of the spine, for which there was no known cure at that time. She had spent months lying in hospital, interspersed with spells of relatively normal living, of which this was one. Sheila spoke openly of having contemplated suicide. In spite of all this, she found time to act as a counsellor and adviser to people suffering from obsessional over-eating, and was even writing a book on the subject. A week previously she had come up north to have a serious operation at Shotley Bridge Hospital, but for some reason there was a delay. Sheila had decided to spend the week enjoying the countryside, as she knew her parents would wrap her in cotton wool if she went home. Although in constant pain, she was at least enjoying herself in her own way,

A horse near Trows Farm on the last day of my Pennine Way walk. (Author's collection)

going each day for long walks in the forest on her own. She had that intensity about her characteristic of those whose days are numbered, and she spoke with great enthusiasm of such things as the smell of decaying spruce needles. There was a gleam shining through her personality to which I can only give the name of genius.

After the meal we stepped outside. The evening was still light and warm. Sheila insisted that it was too beautiful to stay indoors, so we went to the hotel for a drink, and then walked a short way into the forest.

By the time I got up next morning Sheila was already off, walking through the forest footpath towards Kielder and no doubt relishing those natural sights, sounds and smells she loved so well. I never saw her again, but the memory of those few hours I spent in her company will always be with me.

Joe Hutton was the farmer at Rowhope Farm where I spent the following night. It was a sheep farm set at the foot of the beautiful Rowhope Valley, and boasting six hundred black-faced Swaledales. I remember well the descent to the farm. Windy

Gyle was in front of me, its southern spur forming the east side of the valley. At a summit named Mazie Law I turned south-west and followed a broad grassy ridge known as 'the Street'. Near a ruined cottage I joined a narrow, winding sheep track, and then at last the farm appeared: a black shed; the stone-built house; a sycamore; and a girl in a pink dress hanging out some washing. A lamb appeared to like my company – it followed me through two gates, and when Mrs Hutton opened the door it jumped straight in!

Joe Hutton's main claim to fame was as a performer on the Northumbrian pipes, which he had started playing as long ago as 1935. He made a big contribution to the revival of interest in this instrument, won many competitions and produced some fine records. As we ate our evening meal in the dining room, Joe's silver cups near the window gleamed in the early evening sunlight. After the meal we went into the living room and Joe played a cassette recording of traditional tunes made by himself and George Hepple, a fiddler from Haltwhistle. I remember especially 'Derwentwater's Lament'. Each time I named a tune Joe would give me a knowing wink.

Then came my last day on the Pennine Way, passing Windy Gyle, the Hen Hole Gorge and the final rocky summit, the Schil. Towards the end there was a feeling of both pleasure and regret in going down those last few miles to Kirk Yetholm. I couldn't quite understand my feelings as I descended the steep path into the Trowup Valley, and walked that final stretch of lane, its verges bright with broom, whitethorn, vetch, vetchling and clover.

Border Hotel, Kirk Yetholm: the end of the Pennine Way. (Author's collection)

A portrait of Susan Sunderland attributed to Samuel Howell; her looks are as queenly as her singing. (Courtesy of Huddersfield Choral Society)

7

Music

Back home at Thurstonland there was something of a feeling of anticlimax. I had mementos, of course: the mud-stains on my copy of Wainwright; the little piece of purple fluorspar picked up on a Cross Fell spoil-heap, and now adorning the mantelpiece; a few heather cuttings in the propagating case; about a hundred and seventy photographic slides; and, most precious of all, the memory – the one thing that nothing but death can take away from you.

Then on the following Monday it was back to the Music Library, to face once more the criticism that we had no records of the world's greatest pianist (Liberace, apparently), to sort out choirs who had joined forces for a concert and mixed up all their copies, and generally to cope with the petty annoyances which are the common lot of a music librarian. Summer tends to bring something of a lull in Yorkshire's musical activities, but there is no real let-up. There will be concerts in the fine local country churches, with young lady music students in diaphanous white dresses giving a passably convincing impression of being angelic. As autumn approaches the concerts lie with increasing thickness in one's diary until one day there is a distinct nip in the air – and we know that *Messiah* time is again upon us!

What makes some areas especially musical – such as the industrial valleys of South Wales and West Yorkshire? (For many years all I knew of Huddersfield was that it had a choral society that was renowned for the way it thundered through the 'Hallelujah Chorus'). One theory once put to me was that such musical development was due to the puritan, nonconformist influence. Drinking and womanising were out, so what was there left to do? Singing and general music-making was apparently the obvious answer. The main objection to this theory seems to be the way in which drinking, womanising and music often run alongside one another as a perfectly harmonious trio.

Be that as it may, the roots of the tradition go back a long time, much earlier than the official founding-dates of existing societies would indicate. No doubt in good Queen Bess's glorious days, when England was 'a nest of singing birds', the madrigals would have sounded out as loud and clear in Yorkshire as elsewhere. In churches, and later (with the coming of nonconformity) in chapels, the local stalwarts undoubtedly goaded their vocal chords into many a resounding performance. Unfortunately this earlier period is largely unrecorded, or the records thereof are scattered, most local musical historians being primarily concerned with their own particular society.

Even the history of the societies themselves is complex and confusing. When you read of the Huddersfield Glee Club flourishing in the 1820s, you might reasonably assume this was synonymous with the later Huddersfield Glee and Madrigal Society. But no. The latter wasn't founded until 1875 and, to make matters even more puzzling, they eventually changed their name to the Huddersfield Singers. (Perhaps the library staff, who habitually referred to them as 'the Glee and Mad', had some influence on this decision!)

But of course far and away the most famous musical society in the area (as far as the outside world is concerned) is the Huddersfield Choral Society,* which owes its origin to a meeting at the Plough Inn on 7 June 1836, when sixteen gentlemen 'agreed to establish a Musical Society, to be called "The Huddersfield Choral Society"'. They further went on to declare that future gatherings were to be held at the Infants School in Spring Street, on the Friday of or before the full moon of each month. (The town centre had in fact had gas lighting since 1822, but the full moon would be important to members travelling in from a distance.)

Although the sixteen persons at the inaugural meeting were all male, it is obvious that ladies took an important part almost from the beginning. The most famous of them was Susan Sunderland, who later became the legendary 'Yorkshire Queen of Song'. She came from Brighouse and was the daughter of a gardener. Her musical gifts were discovered when she was 12 by a local blacksmith, Luke Settle, who invited her down to his forge and taught her to sing, beating out the rhythms on his anvil! In December 1836, when for the first time the Society sang extracts from *Messiah*, Susan, now aged 17, sang the soprano solos. Two years later she married Henry Sunderland, a butcher by trade, who seems to have been a somewhat shadowy figure. She ceased to be an ordinary member in 1845, and might thereafter be described as an extraordinary member, for she returned many times in her capacity as a famous soloist. Apart from her musical gifts, Susan was also a great walker, often walking to the concert, singing her demanding solos, and then walking back home afterwards. In June 1888 there was a big concert in Brighouse to celebrate Henry and Susan Sunderland's Golden Wedding, and following on from this celebration a committee was set up to inaugurate a musical competition in her honour. Thanks to this, Susan Sunderland is known by name at least to all local music-lovers, with the eponymous competition brightening up the dull days of February every year. Alas, sound-recording came too late to capture her voice, so we only have the praises of her contemporaries to go on. Her portrait, attributed to Samuel Howell, shows that Susan Sunderland's looks were as queenly as her singing.

In those early days, when the aesthetic members were sampling the beauty of Susan's voice, the more pedantic were busy drawing up rules and regulations. One

* This section is largely based on Robert Edwards's book, *And the Glory: A History in Commemoration of the 150th Anniversary of the Huddersfield Choral Society* (Maney, 1985).

Huddersfield Town Hall. (Author's collection)

of these has achieved a certain immortality in its own right – namely 'that no person shall be a member of this Society, who frequents the Hall of Science or any of the Socialist Meetings . . . nor shall the Librarian be allowed to lend any copies of Music belonging to this Society to any Socialist upon pain of expulsion'.

The Hall of Science in Bath Street* was then a centre for those of a radical persuasion, and in particular for the supporters of Robert Owen. Rightly or wrongly, the Choral Society saw it as a den of atheistical socialism. And the rule contained by no means empty words, for a year later one William Littlewood was suitably reprimanded by the chairman for having attended a gathering at the dreaded establishment. I am uncertain whether this rule against socialists was ever rescinded, or has merely fallen into disuse. However, I think we can assume that the spiritual fervour of the 'Hallelujah Chorus' isn't entirely produced by Tories, Liberals and Don't Knows!

All this of course relates to the early years of the Society, and many significant things lay ahead. In 1881 Huddersfield Town Hall was built. It is hard now to imagine the Choral Society and this building as not coexisting from the beginning. Four years later they had the good fortune to engage the services of the brilliant and energetic young conductor John North, who, interestingly enough to me now, was also conductor of Todmorden Choral Society.** Alas, North died of typhoid fever at the early age of 39. His successor, John Bowling, was a competent musician who apparently had only one fault – namely, that he couldn't conduct! He was persuaded to resign in 1901.

---

* The building still stands, and is the premises of Ramsay Clay. Until fairly recently the words 'Hall of Science' could still be made out, but they have now been obliterated.

** Unfortunately, there isn't a continuous history with the present Todmorden Choral Society.

It is extraordinary that the period from 1901 to 1967 was spanned by only two conductors, both of them remarkable musicians: Sir Henry Coward (1901–32) and Sir Malcolm Sargent (1932–67). The latter years of Sargent's reign were a golden age, and certainly the time of the Society's greatest fame outside Huddersfield. Even Vienna, that most musical of cities, offered the choir its warmest accolades. At the two concerts given there in the summer of 1958, the first of *Messiah*, and the second comprising 'Belshazzar's Feast' and Fauré's 'Requiem', the cheering and applauding continued for fifteen minutes and was still going on after the orchestral players had crept away.

Looking now at the list of works performed by the Choral Society over the years, you inevitably see those great war-horses that have been trotted out over and over again: *The Creation, Elijah* and above all *Messiah*. It seems that however many times the Society's finances went into the red, it could be – and was – rescued yet again by another performance of Handel's ubiquitous masterpiece. The list also contains works that were composed long ago but not performed until relatively recently, such as Bruckner's *F minor Mass*, surely one of the most beautiful of all choral works. Written in 1868, this work was not performed until 1970, so slow were the British to appreciate the great Austrian master. Lastly there are those pieces that were once popular but are now, perhaps unjustly, left to gather dust.

When I first started work at the Music Library I soon became aware of the remnants of this third category. They were gathering dust in both the metaphorical and the literal sense, so much so in fact that the entire room exuded a curious odour. I came across multiple copies of Michael Costa's oratorio *Eli*, a work I had not previously heard of, but which the Society had sung three times in the nineteenth century but never in the twentieth. Despite this, the copies were still kept on the open shelves. The thirty or so copies of Sullivan's *The Golden Legend* were, however, confined to the library stack, where they remained so totally undisturbed that when it was decided to transfer them to the large music library at Wakefield, it was found that they had congealed into a solid mass and had to be chipped apart!

And there were other fossilised relics of musical history, such as the gigantic full scores of the three parts of Joseph Holbrooke's *The Cauldron of Annwyn*, a work that rivals Wagner's *The Ring of the Nibelung* in scale, though probably not in quality. The volumes were indeed immense, and I can remember one of them once accidentally crashing to the bottom of the lift-shaft. What on earth were they doing at Huddersfield? My friend Ron Phillips came up with the explanation. It seems that whereas the first two parts of the trilogy (*The Children of Don* and *Dylan, Son of the Wave*) had received performances in both London and Vienna, the final part, *Bronwen*, was only staged once, at the Theatre Royal at Huddersfield in 1929. The production was sponsored by the local parish organist Eaglefield Hull, and was the subject of much wrangling, to the extent that in the end Holbrooke refused to have anything to do with it.

Eaglefield Hull himself was obviously a fascinating character, and had left his mark on the Music Library, many of the scores bearing his autograph on the flyleaf. In addition to being an organist, he was a musicologist, and the author of several textbooks on composition as well as studies of various composers. I remember the journalist Sidney Crowther telling me of a visit he once paid to Franz Lehar. When he arrived Lehar was out, but he met a young American student who was having composition lessons from the great master of Viennese operetta. Sidney asked what textbook they were using, and lo and behold it turned out to be Eaglefield Hull's.

Hull seems to have had a photographic memory, and in a rather bizarre way this led to his death. Among his writings is a study of Scriabin, and it seems that he incorporated into it some of the ideas of Friedrich Blume, reproducing whole passages almost verbatim, without apparently being aware of their origin. He chanced to be reading a review of his book on Huddersfield railway station, in which the reviewer had pointed out this unintended plagiarism. On an impulse Hull threw himself under a passing train. He survived the accident, but sadly died later from his injuries.

In any account of the musical history of Huddersfield the names of the performing musicians are likely to recur most often, especially Susan Sunderland, George Stead (who conducted the Colne Valley Male Voice Choir for over forty years) and the violinist Rodney Friend. Composers are unlikely to feature much, although the area has had its share. Drivers on the ring-road are likely to be too absorbed in the traffic to notice the inconspicuous monument to Sir Walter Parratt (1841–1924) near the fire station, but Parratt was a remarkable man. He was the son of Thomas Parratt, who served as organist at Huddersfield parish church for fifty years, from 1812 to 1862. The young Walter was so precocious that at 12 years old he could play the whole of Bach's 'Well-tempered clavier' from memory. A distinguished career was crowned by his appointment as Master of the Queen's Music in 1893 (he was the immediate predecessor of Sir Edward Elgar in the post). Parratt's compositions include sacred works, incidental music for plays, and songs. Also largely forgotten is Sir Edward Bairstow (1874–1946), who spent many years as organist at York Minster. His church music is still sometimes performed. Neither should contemporary composers associated with the area be overlooked, such as Richard Steinitz and Arthur Butterworth.

In a town with such strong traditions there is bound to be a measure of cultural conservatism. I remember being told by one member of the Choral Society that some of his fellow singers considered that musical history began with the births of Bach and Handel (1685) and ended with the death of Brahms (1897), and that everything on either side was only fit for the litter bin. No doubt this was an exaggeration, but I gather that Carl Orff's *Carmina Burana* and David Fanshawe's *African Sanctus* were selected for performance in the face of considerable opposition.

In view of this philistinism, it is perhaps surprising that Huddersfield should have become the home of a Contemporary Music Festival. That this came to pass would seem to have been due largely to the enthusiasm and dedication of one man, Richard Steinitz. It started in 1978 in a very small way, but soon developed into an event of international importance. A list of the composers who have taken part is virtually a roll-call of all the eminent composers of our time: Boulez, Messiaen,

Cage, Stockhausen, Part, Adams, Reich, Birtwistle, Tippett and Berio. Each year the programme seems to get fatter and fatter, with performances taking place at all times of the day and night.

But the modern element didn't make its inroads without incurring a few snide remarks. I was once present at a recital in the Town Hall Reception Room at which Ron Newton performed a piece for prepared piano by the American composer John Cage. This was quite a visual experience as well as an aural one, as we watched various objects which looked like clothes pegs, paper clips and hairpins – being inserted into the piano strings. The piece was then performed, whereupon the process was reversed – sundry items being accidentally twanged across the room as the piano was restored to its normal condition. All seemed to have gone well. The work had been listened to respectfully, and a moderate volume of applause was accorded to it at the end. A few days later, however, a lady from the suburb of Lindley who I had seen at the recital entered the Music Library. After a few general remarks she came up to the counter and said: 'This chap John Cage – is he some sort of teacher at the School of Music'?

'Oh no,' I replied, 'he's a composer with an international reputation.'

The lady grunted sarcastically. 'Well, it hasn't reached Lindley yet!'

Poetry

While John Cage's reputation was struggling manfully up the long hill to Lindley, other branches of culture were meeting with more success, in particular poetry. But in order to understand these developments we need to stand back a bit and think about poetry in a more general sense. The great British public's attitude to poetry is an ambivalent affair. If I ever lingered by the library's out-counter, watching the latest pretty young assistant date-stamping the out-going cowboys, romances, detective stories, etc., the sight of a poetry book passing through her slim hands was something of an event – enough to make me lift my eyes for a moment to examine the curious creature who was borrowing it, or perhaps even to wait until that person was safely out of the door, and then grab the ticket and make a mental note of the name. I never remember seeing any statistics on the subject, but I would guess that about one in every hundred books leaving a typical public library is a poetry book – though even this may be too optimistic.

Yet there is another side to all this. When it comes to a leaving do, a wedding or an engagement party, lo and behold some local bard will emerge and produce a poem which does a pretty passable job of combining rhyme, rhythm and wit. But the creator of this masterpiece will almost certainly disdain being described as a poet.

Poets are (or rather were) thin, pale, aesthetic, long-haired dreamers, looking pathetically at auburn-haired girls and daffodils. And, of course, it went without saying, they were all dead. The idea that we would one day clap eyes on a poet like Ian McMillan – very much alive, and looking more like a professional rugby player – never crossed our minds. At least that seemed to be the state of affairs when I first went to Huddersfield in 1971. Then something happened in the late 1970s or early 1980s – as if at the sound of a trumpet all things were changed. But here I am getting too far ahead.

Even if the Huddersfield area hadn't hitherto been noted for its poetry, the muse had for long been hovering somewhere nearby. Those who visit Almondbury church, and care to crane their necks to inspect the ceiling, can still make out the words of 'The Almondbury Passion' by Geoffrey Dayston (*c.* 1522) – a remarkable piece of verse, written in the persona of Christ on the cross:

> Thou man unkind
> Have in thy mind
> My bloody face

My wounds wide
On every side
For thy trespass . . .

Geoffrey Dayston doesn't appear to have published a collection of poetry. But over the next 450 years poetry was kept alive in a wide variety of ways. Some of the effusions were none too distinguished, such as the 'Lines on the Crosland Moor Train Engine Boiler Explosion June 3rd 1891', and this bit of doggerel from an early twentieth-century postcard:

Here's to good old Huddersfield
Unrivalled in producing
Distinctive goods for many trades
Delighted praise inducing,
Everyone's so full of vim
Regarding work or fun;
Strong in admiration
For their football team, by gum! . . .

But there were far more serious poets around. In the early nineteenth century William Dearden published 'The Death of Leyland's African Bloodhound', 'The Star-Seer' and 'The Vale of Caldene', works that can still be read with pleasure, and are certainly better than those of his erstwhile drinking-companion Branwell Brontë. Later in the century George Calvert composed his *Redemption*, a vast epic that clearly strove to emulate Milton's *Paradise Lost*, but fell somewhat short of its model.

Alongside all this was another rich tradition, that of dialect poetry. West Yorkshire had a long line of eminent practitioners, including Ben Preston, John Hartley and Ben Turner (also remembered as a prominent trade unionist).* The case of Sam Laycock is somewhat curious, since although he was born and died in the Yorkshire village of Marsden most of his life was spent across the great divide, and he is consequently regarded as a Lancashire dialect poet.** When I first moved to Huddersfield one important dialect poet was living close by, although regrettably I never met him and didn't realise his significance until after his death. Fred Brown was born in Keighley in 1893, went to work as a cotton spinner at the age of 13, and died at Crosland Moor in 1979. His best-known poems are contained in *The Muse Went Weaving*, published in 1972. After his death the tradition was carried on by Mollie Baskerville, who, although Irish on both sides, in 'Yah end o't valley' celebrated the Marsden area in its native tongue.

* See Ken Edward Smith's *West Yorkshire Dialect Poets* (Dialect Books, 1982).
** See Kathleen Eyre's *The Real Lancashire* (Dalesman Books, 1983), pp. 82–3.

When I first came to Huddersfield people might have been forgiven for thinking there was but a single poet in the place, Dr Stephen Henderson Smith, although the worthy doctor was more famous for his other pursuits – bee-keeping, kite-flying, violin-playing, writing innumerable letters to the paper, and general eccentricity. Purely as a poet, I don't think he was of the first class, but he did sometimes produce a winner. He was, however, a man of great kindness, and I owe him a very real debt of gratitude.

I also became aware in those early days of Steve Sneyd – sightings of his spare figure and gnomic features were usually made in the dim dusk of the library foyer round about evening closing time. I think I always knew he was a poet, but the friendship between us was slow in growing, being finally clinched when I illustrated his collection *A Mile Beyond the Bus.* There was also Gordon Dyson, physically the exact opposite of Steve – large, cherubic and baby-faced. For about ten years I stamped out his piano scores, without getting anything in return except a strange grunt that I supposed passed for 'thank you'. Then one day a stray remark revealed that we were both not only interested in poetry, but also wrote it.

At that time the only occasion when local poets came together was at the judging of the poetry class in the annual Mrs Sunderland Music Competition. I personally was completely in awe of such events – the idea of meeting people to whom one could confess to writing poetry was both intimidating and liberating. The adjudicator, Norman Butterworth, was very kind and seemed to understand our plight, and always pronounced judgement in the most delicate manner. Then, having exchanged our mutual confidences, we went our separate ways.

I certainly felt the need for something of a more permanent nature. My immediate needs were fulfilled when Dr Henderson Smith introduced me to the Pennine Poets, a group which met (and still meets) at the home of Mabel Ferret at Heckmondwike. The venue, the group and Mabel herself seem inseparable in my thoughts. As with a troop of elephants, so with the Pennine Poets, it is the grand old matriarch who rules. And Mabel's living room (the Poetry Room as I call it) has been the setting for many a stimulating evening.

I remember my first visit on a cold February evening in 1978. I can recollect exactly who was there, and even where they were sitting. It seemed traditional that Brian Merrikin Hill and Stephen Henderson Smith sat in armchairs opposite each other, keeping up a friendly raillery all the while. That first evening Brian read a poem about marram grass, but as so much marram grass gets into his verse I cannot thereby identify it. Ken Edward Smith (who I then confused with 'the other Ken Smith') read 'She dances', which was based on the film *Casablanca.* My contribution was entitled 'In an oppressed country', and Brian immediately asked if he could publish it in *Pennine Platform.* This was very much beginner's luck, and four years were to pass before I had the same good fortune again.

That evening was important to me, in terms both of poetry and of friendships. Looking back on it all from a distance of over twenty years, I can see that Brian Merrikin Hill was probably the finest poet of the group, and it was at this time, fairly late in life, that he was producing his most significant work. Few people have

A poetry reading in the Father Willis Bar, Huddersfield Town Hall, 15 September 1981. From left to right: Mabel McGowan, Gordon Dyson, Trevor Innes and Stephen Henderson Smith. (Courtesy of the Huddersfield Examiner)

expressed so poignantly man's spiritual yearnings – and yet there is an honesty about his writings which does not baulk at admitting the shortcomings of his (and our) understandings. At the time his poetry was little known, but over the next few years a series of collections brought it to the attention of the more discerning. *Wakeful in the sleep of time* is probably the most important of his publications.

A copy of this very book was instrumental in providing a clue as to what would happen next. One day, while passing the lending library counter, I saw *Wakeful in the sleep of time* lying there with a request card sticking out of it. I was sufficiently intrigued to pull out the card and read the name of the requester – Peter Sansom. It meant nothing to me then, but I was to hear that name many times in the succeeding years.

During the winter of 1980/1, as Secretary of Kirklees Arts Council, I arranged a series of poetry readings, most of which took place in the Father Willis Bar of the Town Hall. Some included a musical item as well – I remember Pete Norman playing the bowed psaltery. For the last of them we had Adrian Henri. Leaflets were placed on the seats asking people if they wanted a more permanent event. The upshot of this was the founding of the Kirklees Poetry Society in the autumn of 1981. The powers that be gave their blessing, the Director of Yorkshire Arts (Michael Dawson) and the chief of Kirklees Libraries and Arts (Brian Pearson) being present. I was elected Chairman.

It was shortly after this that Peter Sansom began his poetic activities at the Polytechnic, and thereafter poetry began to spread like an epidemic. Peter seemed to have endless energy and enthusiasm, and had soon gathered around himself a considerable following, consisting mainly (but not entirely) of young people. Instead of the meagre audiences which had hitherto been the norm, poetry events that were organised in the Art Gallery and elsewhere were absolutely packed out. I remember Peter standing at the counter of the Music Library one evening, and telling me about a young lad from Marsden named Simon Armitage who had been coming to his workshops. 'We're certainly going to hear more about him,' Peter said. This wasn't actually the first time I'd heard mention of the Armitage family, since a few years previously I'd listened to Simon's grandfather giving a rendition of 'Albert and the Lion' at the Marsden Band Room.

By the late 1980s I was aware that almost everybody in Huddersfield was writing poetry (or so it seemed). No longer was it a secretive activity for the closet – to be a poet was the 'in thing'. Although this was true of the whole community, it was especially so with the younger generation, those in their late teens and early 20s. I was also aware by this time that in a curious way which no one had intended or foreseen the members of the Kirklees Poetry Society came to be seen as the 'fuddy duddies' of the poetic scene. This was certainly not because of any opposition from Peter Sansom; in fact, he was on our committee. But by the late 1980s things were beginning to look bad for us: attendances at meetings fluctuated wildly, according to the popularity of the guest poet, and we lacked a steady following. We were also low on cash. When in early 1989 we had an application for a grant from Kirklees turned down, we felt there was nothing for it but to fold. On 11 May of that year we held an annual general meeting which was basically a valediction. Peter actually pressed for us to carry on, but with next to nothing in the kitty it was difficult to see how this was to be achieved.

However, this proved to be a fairly minor hitch in the ongoing developments which led to Huddersfield being described (half-jokingly at first) as the 'Poetry Capital of England'. I think I'm right in seeing Peter Sansom as the central figure in this. Leading on from his work at the Polytechnic, he went on to found the publishing imprint of Smith/Doorstop. Their early productions were virtually two books in one, the first being a mini-collection by Simon Armitage entitled *Human Geography*, coupled with *The Hot Blizzard* by Clare Chapman, who I already knew through the Pennine Poets. This was followed by similar volumes linking Steve Hobson with Duncan Curry, and Phil Kendall with Linda Williams. The layout and design of these books was pretty basic, although later on they went in for a far more attractive appearance.

The Byram Arcade, Huddersfield. There was something conspiratorial about the place, as you climbed the long steps to 'The Poetry Business'. (Author's collection)

1. David Quirke, *View from Bare Bones Road down the Holme Valley*, oil on board. (David Quirke)

2. David Quirke, *Dandelion Clocks no. 2*, oil on board. *(David Quirke)*

3. Mary Lord, *Yorkshire Moonlight*, oil on board. *(Photograph Richard Littlewood, courtesy of Sheeran Lock Ltd)*

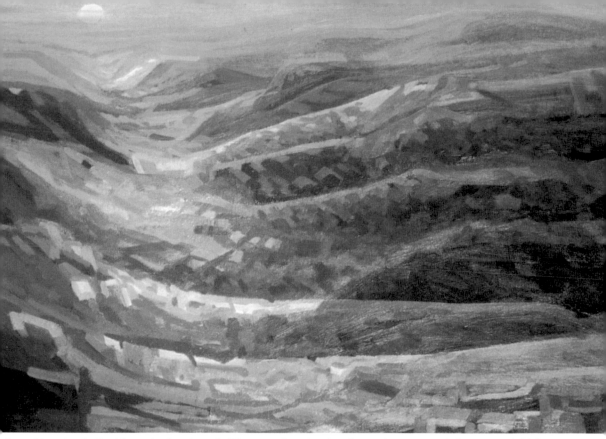

4. Mary Lord, *Cool Sunset*, oil on board. *(Photograph Richard Littlewood, courtesy of Sheeran Lock Ltd)*

5. Mary Lord, *Cool Summer Landscape*, oil on paper. *(Photograph Richard Littlewood, courtesy of Sheeran Lock Ltd)*

6. Mark Murphy, *Pitts Shore, Cornholme, Autumn*, pastel and charcoal. *(Mark Murphy)*

7. Mark Murphy, *Boulder Clough from the Burnley Road between Sowerby Bridge and Luddendenfoot*, acrylic on paper. *(Mark Murphy)*

8. Mark Murphy, *Chiserley and Old Town above Hebden Bridge – from Little Moor*, oil on board. *(Mark Murphy)*

9. Bohuslav Barlow, *Elegy to Bowed Court*, oil on canvas. *(Bohuslav Barlow)*

10. Bohuslav Barlow, *Back to Back*, oil on canvas. (Bohuslav Barlow)

11. Bohuslav Barlow, *Out in the Cold*, pastel. *(Bohuslav Barlow)*

12. Shanti Dutta, *Blue Maiden*, oil on board. *(Photograph Anthony Mellor)*

13. David Quirke, *Tree study – Lumb Bank*, pastel. *(David Quirke)*

Peter's next venture was The Poetry Business, a centre for poetry and poets established on the top floor of the Byram Arcade. One felt there was something conspiratorial about the place, as you climbed the long steps of the ornate Victorian building and found yourself in the sacred precincts, the walls lined with poetry books, the tables scattered over with magazines, Janet Fisher bashing furtively at the typewriter, and some disconsolate poet slumped in an old armchair, gathering strength and inspiration for his next sally into the cruel world beyond – where booksellers and publishers seemed interested in nothing except making money.

The sequence of events is now a bit blurred in my memory. I can remember various workshops held in this esoteric setting, and also (I think at a somewhat later date) in the luxurious ambience of the staff bar at the Polytechnic. This came to an abrupt halt, however, when we fell under suspicion of stealing billiard balls from the adjoining tables! We in our turn pointed the finger of accusation at a young gentleman who had appeared at one of our gatherings, read a rather clever rhyming poem, and had never been seen again. It seemed a rather unlikely branch of criminal activity for poets to get involved in, and to the best of my knowledge the mystery remains unsolved. But the upshot was that we were banished to a rather dreary class-room on the floor below.

All that I have written in this chapter merely describes the early years of the poetic revolution in Huddersfield. If the story is to be continued it must be written by someone else, since, for reasons that I will give later, after about 1989 I was spending less and less time in the area. I can here only give indications of later developments: the Huddersfield Poetry Festival, the Word Hoard, the Literature Resource Centre and the remarkably crowded gatherings of the Albert Poets. Many gifted individuals were drawn into this cultural mêlée: burly Geoff Hattersley (who combines poetry with his work as a machine operator), Keith Jafrate (a noted saxophonist as well as a poet), Milner Place (looking very much the retired sea-captain), David Morley, Stephanie Bowgett, John Bosley, John Duffy and many others. As Steve Sneyd once said, 'If an asteroid hit Huddersfield, the chances of it killing a poet would be very high.'

Auden has written that 'Poetry makes nothing happen'. In Huddersfield, during the period of which I speak, poetry certainly made many things happen. Perhaps Shelley was nearer the mark when he described poets as 'the trumpets which sing to battle . . .'.

9

Landscape

Climb to the top of any summit in the West Yorkshire Pennines, and you will see much the same view: in almost every direction long, grey, flattish hilltops, with brief breaks for cloughs and valleys. It may be called the Pennine Chain, but this is no chain of mountains – just one vast eroded plateau stretching north and south, largely composed (as far as West Yorkshire is concerned) of millstone grit. How different is the east of Yorkshire, with the undulating Wolds – a vivid green veneer above chalky whiteness, and with violent yellow splashes from the fields of oilseed rape, or the Vale of York, which, when viewed from the edge of the Wolds at Garrowby Hill, appears to stretch forever, with its flat pattern of fields and its slow rivers, meandering, converging, changing their names, till they finally disgorge into the North Sea via the broad Humber Estuary.

Artists have interpreted this landscape in their own idiosyncratic way. Like students engaged in life-drawing, they look at the same model, yet portray the subject in a manner that depends on the eye and the mind of the observer. In this chapter I want to take four Yorkshire-based artists, David Quirke, Mary Lord, Mark Murphy and Bohuslav Barlow, and consider their varied reactions to the landscape around them. This selection is purely subjective. I have not been influenced by relative fame (a most fickle and unreliable guide) but simply by the appeal they make to me. All four are highly original, yet I am constantly aware that their work is rooted in a deep love for the scenery they portray.

Strangely enough, three out of my four artists are, like myself, in-comers. David Quirke is half-Irish and half-Welsh (surely a living argument for those who contend that the Celtic fringes are the great power-houses of British creativity). He was born in a rural area in Warwickshire called Newham Paddox, which no doubt exists on some maps, though I have so far failed to find it. He came to Huddersfield at the age of 8, and thereafter his life has been an exploration of many aspects of artistic expression. Music and drama are both important to him: he sings, plays the guitar and composes songs – both words and lyrics. In the visual arts he is equally varied. His exquisite and intimate portrayals of family life must also be mentioned, even although they lie outside the scope of this chapter.

David's originality as a landscape painter lies in what he chooses to see. Scenes that other artists pass by as insignificant, David lingers over and paints with a loving, painstaking exactitude which is never pedantic or tedious. He will look at a hillside covered in trees, where there is no single object standing out to focus on. Yet he will paint it, and somehow make it meaningful. As he himself says, 'The whole scene is in focus.' Or he will take a vast panorama, or a tiny patch of grass with a scattering of wildflowers, and tell us something about these things which we would otherwise have missed.

In his oil painting *View from Bare Bones Road down the Holme Valley* he depicts one of his panoramic views – an area frequently walked over by me and my dog Sooty. It is a scene that one would pause for a moment to admire, but only for its sense of distance, for it is surely rather nondescript. The summer skies above Yorkshire, especially on days of sunshine and showers, can be dramatic – the swift-moving clouds constantly changing shape and colour, the lagoons of sky between them intensely blue. But on that day in late July 1996 when David painted this scene the weather was clearly warm and settled. One long bank of fair-weather cumulus floats across the upper sky, and below it is a hint of brownish-pink – a sure sign of still air. The windmill on the far right is turning very slowly, and a still, warm light suffuses everything. The land in the foreground is poor and too infertile to support anything except those long serried lines of conifers. The intake fields beyond are poor also, barely worth reclaiming. Long and narrow, like the painting itself, their shape harks back to ancient field-divisions, of a type also apparent at Fulstone and Haworth. Left of centre is Holme Styles Reservoir, its unrippled surface a greyish brown. Farms and isolated trees dot the hillsides, and one can just make out the Victoria Tower on Castle Hill. Beyond the distant hills and the lower sky meet in an almost imperceptible line. But yet the picture says something. One looks at it, comes back and looks again, and cannot help but look – and the fascination remains intangible.

Tree study – Lumb Bank is one of David's 'treescapes', this time in pastel. The picture in a sense has no shape – you just see leaves, fragments of twigs and branches, and bits of trunk unobscured by leaves. But when one has looked for a while various things emerge: one senses the steep sloping hillside beneath the tree canopy, running from upper right to lower left, and the struggle of every branch and leaf to surge upwards towards the light. It is not abstract painting, but it offers some of the pleasures of abstract painting, notably in the subtle grouping of numerous variants of green. But over and above this, it gives a joy which purely abstract painting never can: it is a glorification of the superabundance of nature, of nature's own creativity.

Another body of David's work portrays what one might call 'mini-landscapes', in which he depicts a few feet of ground, the sort of area one might glance at while walking along. There's a clump of rosebay willow herb out of season, the leaves turning reddish-orange, with the fluffy inflorescences standing out against a background of dark green; or a group of poppies, splashes of red splattered over the chalky fields of the Yorkshire Wolds. *Dandelion Clocks no. 2* is another of these mini-landscapes. The tiny ridges of the grassland seem to imitate the long grey-green ridges of the Pennines themselves. Dotted around are the dandelions, some still in yellow flower, others already turned to clocks. As one looks at the painting they form into random patterns, as stars do to an observer on a clear night.

In one of his intimate family studies David portrays himself beyond a window, his daughter Eve held in his left arm. With his right hand he points forward. This is a synonym for all his work: with each drawing and painting he is saying, 'Look, see this – and this.'

David Quirke's approach is fairly traditional in that having selected his unusual viewpoint, his actual depiction is precisely representational. My other three artists all seem to absorb the landscape into themselves, and then reinvent it. Mary Lord is the only one of the quartet with her roots firmly in the Yorkshire soil. She was born at Birstall in 1931, and both her father and grandfather had been amateur artists. Her life has obviously been something of a struggle to balance the inner creative urge with the need to earn a living. Although she has painted since childhood, Mary seems to have explored various interesting byways before coming to her own distinctive landscape manner.

As a child she apparently had the curious habit of making papier mâché models of the places visited by the family. This seems prophetic of her later style. Some of these mature pictures remind me of those dioramas you sometimes see in museums, laying bare the basic geological structure of a scene. Such a picture is *Yorkshire Moonlight*, painted in oils in 1990. Here we look out of a window: there is a hint of curtains on either side, and some dull-reddish flowers in a vase slightly left of centre. Beyond all this is the true subject: the landscape. First, there's a small village set on a descending slope; it is sketched in hastily, merely a feeling of moonlight on the roofs and chimney-stacks. Above the village we see the valley, a long meandering Yorkshire dale, with a dark V-shaped centre, and wide 'shelves' stretching up to the tops, and higher still the sky of vibrant tossing clouds, the whole suffused with an exquisite blue. Is there a full moon somewhere behind the clouds at the top left? I'm not sure. Another ambiguous thing about the painting is that although it contains not a single living creature, it doesn't appear dehumanised: there is a sense that the flowers in the window are cared for, and that each home in the small village houses some sleeping inhabitants.

I spoke earlier of the Pennines as 'grey', but of course they are only grey (or bluey-grey) if seen from a distance. When you actually walk on the tops, the landscape is full of subtle colouring: the predominant hue of the coarse grass is a dull green, but here and there are patches of rust-red Yorkshire fog, while bilberry adds a touch of a lighter, fresher green. Dark greens are provided by crowberry and bracken, and down in the wet soggy hollows the stands of reed are darker still. Climb in late winter to such a summit as the curiously named Harbour Hill near Haworth, and you will probably see little except drab browns and greens – but go up in September and the slopes are covered in the purple glow of heather.

Mary Lord captures something of this in *Cool Sunset*. Once again a valley features largely, this time running across the picture from top left to bottom right. Just above the valley's head the sun is half-obscured by a long strand of horizontal cloud, as it dips below the moorland. In those last few minutes before setting, it lights up the long spurs that run from the tops to the valley bottom, and each one is coloured slightly differently: touches of pink, of brown, of several shades of green; and in the nearer spurs there is an increasingly intense sense of shadow, with dull bluey-greens verging towards black. And again there is a foreground village, its roofs a reddish brown, lit by the last fading rays of dusk.

But some of Mary Lord's most exciting works are not finished paintings – they are her so-called 'loose beginnings'. These are preparatory sketches, which, despite the artist's own opinion, I think can be regarded as works of art fully satisfying in themselves. In *Cool Summer Landscape* we see yet another valley, but now we are on a lower stretch, with the base broadened out and the floor dotted with trees. Maybe it was painted in just a few minutes, but how unified it is: the few brushstrokes in blue and grey that represent the sky are echoed by the long sweeps of pale green, brown and blackish-blue depicting the wide valley floor. In the far background are the hills, the one to the right of centre being slightly more pointed than most of the Pennines – is it West Nab above Meltham? I don't know, and in a way it doesn't matter. Mary's pictures disdain the precise and the actual in favour of the generalised emotion generated by the scene. Despite the lack of figures, this all-embracing feeling somehow humanises her pictures.

This absence of living things links Mary Lord with our next artist, Mark Murphy, but here the resemblance ends. There is a placidity about Mary Lord's paintings, but to stand in the midst of one of Mark Murphy's exhibitions is to be aware of some disturbing inexorable downward movement, driving all things by its impetus. Over and over he portrays the cloughs, those short, steep valleys cutting into the Pennines. There may be a glimpse of sky – but only a glimpse – and likewise a glimpse of the edge of the moors. But mostly he is interested in the sloping sides, and his pictures have a 'downward plunging' feeling. You can sense the centuries of rainstorms which have carved out those slopes as you gaze at the exposed rocks, the steep sheep-grazed fields, and the narrow valleys where water-power ruled as the forerunner of modern industry.

Mark was born in 1952 at Welwyn Garden City, of all unlikely places! (I worked at the library there for three years from 1957 to 1960, and like to nurture the illusion that I helped Mark to choose a book in the junior library as a small boy.) Anything more remote from his pictures than the polite cherry-fringed avenues of a garden city it would be hard to imagine. He first saw the Pennines in 1971, when he was a student at Liverpool School of Art, and travelled by train to Leeds via the line which runs up the Saddleworth Valley, through the Stannage Tunnel and out into the Colne Valley at Marsden. His first reaction was that this was a scarred landscape. Like a human face, it bore the marks of past joy and suffering. It also tied up with something he intuitively wanted to do in his art.

For some years Mark was obsessed with the area known as Pitts Shore, which lies on the north-east side of the Burnley Valley above Cornholme, close to the Lancashire border. One of the fruits of this obsession was a large pastel entitled *Pitts Shore, Cornholme, Autumn*. From a distance one might mistake it for an oil painting, but no, the whole effect is conveyed with bold forceful strokes of pastel. This is very much one of his 'downward plunging' pictures. In the sky the white clouds seem to be falling into the neck of the high clough. Against the clouds stand the white three-armed windmills; they are merely sketched in, yet somehow you know there is a high wind and the sails are turning wildly. Below the windmills the plunging movement continues: the edge of the high moors curves down over broken rocks, where autumnal trees glint orange in the late afternoon sunlight; the luminous greens of the steeply sloping fields and the greys of the stone walls emphasise strong diagonals, which are broken only by the verticals of telegraph poles. All this appears in vivid colours. Only the bottom left-hand corner is truly dark, where the down-sweeping waters have washed everything into blackness.

The long title of his next painting, *Boulder Clough from the Burnley Road between Sowerby Bridge and Luddendenfoot*, suggests a very precise location. But here there is no precision. What is glorified is the essential, the generalised. This is a celebration of the numerous side valleys which reach down from the high peaty Pennine moors to the steep small fields of the lower slopes. The hills beyond are such as formed the background to Emily Brontë's *Wuthering Heights*, and the poems Ted Hughes gathered together in *Remains of Elmet*. From these brown hills 'fifteen wild Decembers [and many more] have melted into spring . . .'. The waters from the melting snows on the high tops have made these less elevated regions lush and intense with greens and browns and blues. But despite the vividness, this is a sombre picture. A melancholy broods over everything, 'a presence which is not to be put by . . .'.

Light has come into the world in *Chiserley and Old Town above Hebden Bridge, from Little Moor*, despite the season being winter. This is one of those clear November afternoons, when the low-lying sunlight brings into relief all the cracks and wrinkles of the hillside. Natural and artificial blur together, the old quarries and spoil heaps and the rolling hills and tiny wooded cloughs. The exhausted traveller, back from his tramp through the heather and cotton grass, sees beyond his tiredness the colours of premature twilight, the creams and greens and reddish-browns. The sheds in the foreground hint at some human activity, but no being enlivens the scene. Everything is merely glimpsed through a 'wilting dusk of weariness'.

How different from this is the highly figurative world of Bohuslav Barlow! It is as if he has to swallow up the landscape, then regurgitate it completely changed. The erstwhile level viaducts are tipped to a skittish angle, chimney pots stand on their heads, and the already-leaning houses of Todmorden lean even further. And on to this bizarre stage he brings his troupe of players: rocking horses, clowns, starfish, puppets and beautiful nude women.

Bohuslav's life-story is almost as remarkable as his paintings. He was born at Bruntal, a small peasant township in Upper Moravia, in Czechoslovakia in 1947, just as the 'iron curtain' was descending. The story of the next twenty-odd years is one of much hardship and frustration. Being exiled from his roots, he had to invent a basic mythology all of his own. Like Mark Murphy, he regards his first sight of the West Yorkshire landscape as a realisation of his true pathway as an artist. Into that landscape he poured his own curious individual myths.

At 26 he came to Todmorden and first settled at Bowed Court, a row of cottages built at a spot where Eagle Crag appears to be leaping into flight above the infant River Calder, a place much eulogised two hundred years earlier by the weaver-poet Samuel Law. In 1981 Barlow commemorated this part of his life in one of his most magical paintings, *Elegy to Bowed Court*. In the foreground a beautiful nude girl bends over two puppets, one slouched on a chair, the other collapsed forwards, dropping a violin and its bow in the process, in a visual pun on the place-name. Beyond, a line of steps ascends from the courtyard to a field, and in the far background is Eagle Crag, with the slope of the valley beneath it, and a threatening sky above. It is a picture of subdued tones and the merest hint of colour – only the field and the girl's body receive much light. The form is based on diagonals: the valley side, the steps and the line of figures; with a post and the violin stabbing it with a couple of verticals. But what does it all mean? The girl, who has inspired so much, looks perplexedly at the broken-down puppets. The violin will not play again, the dog's bowl is empty, a magpie and some chickens can only peck at the merest crumbs. But there is hope. The exquisite body of the girl and the sublimity of the distant landscape point to eventual regeneration.

In contrast, *Back to Back* takes us up on to the rocky edge of the moors overlooking the valley. The location is a group of rocks known as 'The Bridestones' (also the subject of a poem by Ted Hughes*). The remarkably shaped Bridestone itself is largely obscured in this picture, but prominent in the top left-hand corner is a rock which I have privately nicknamed 'The Barrel'. In front of this a nude man and woman sit back to back, as the title implies. Bohuslav usually portrays the naked body as soft and sensuous, but in this case the figures are depicted with a certain coarse roughness, as if akin to the rocks behind them. But the facial expressions are tender. The woman cradles in her arms a bundle of cloth – or is it a baby? One isn't quite sure. Despite the back-to-back position, you feel there is no quarrel between these two. They seem to share the same serene meditation, which links them to the rocks, the moors, the sky – and to each other. In his book *Visual Alchemy*, Barlow has chosen to put a quotation from Wordsworth opposite this picture: 'The world is too much with us, late and soon,/Getting and spending we lay waste our powers.' The painting reminds us of those powers we are in danger of losing: the love that binds us to our fellow human beings, and to the natural world of which we are inescapably a part.

The next picture takes us back to the valley floor. *Out in the Cold* is in pastel. For background there is a cold moon in a wintry sky, shining down on white clouds, dark grey moors, a mill, some chimneys and a row of houses. In the foreground two lovers cling to each other. They have been driven out by an unfeeling world, and can only find comfort in the mutual warmth of their bodies. But are they human beings? Are they puppets? Are they people dressed as puppets? Whatever they are, unlike the couple in *Back to Back* they are not at one with their surroundings. The theme of this picture is alienation.

The setting of *Out in the Cold* is Lydgate, an old mill village wedged in one of the narrowest parts of the upper Calder Valley. It is interesting to reflect that the location is very close to Mark Murphy's *Pitts Shore, Cornholme, Autumn*, considered earlier. Thus the same model reclines, the same light falls on her body; only the mind of the artist creates the variations.

* See Ted Hughes, *Remains of Elmet*, with photographs by Fay Godwin (Faber, 1979), p. 64.

10

Bright Sari in a Darkened Street

It is an autumn evening; the street lights are coming on. The young Hindu girl in the cerise sari walks down the cracked millstone pavement, clutching with her right hand at the hem of her sari, holding it fractionally above the dirt and dust. She must be going somewhere very special to be dressed like that: a tika on her forehead, a jewel in her hair, green glittering earrings, gold-sparkling bangles on her slender wrists. The cerise sari – how brightly it contrasts with the drab grey terraced houses on either side of the narrow street. From an open window comes the clatter of cooking utensils, and the smell of pilau wafts on the air. In a side

Shanti Dutta. (Courtesy of the *Huddersfield Examiner*)

alley an old lady unpegs some blue kurtas from a washing line. Further up the pavement three little Sikh boys with guttees on their heads are playing some sort of hopping game – not hopscotch, something else. Nearby stands a tiny Hindu girl in a green kurta and salwar, just looking; and two little white (or rather off-white) boys romp on the kerbstones with grime all over their faces. But it is the girl in the cerise sari who catches the eye. A car stops. A small family inside make room for her on the back seat. She hitches up her sari and thankfully gets in. The car drives off, perhaps to a festival?

It was townscapes such as this which I came to love as I wandered round the back streets of Huddersfield, especially Springwood and Thornton Lodge. And all this was linked in my mind with a remarkable lady whom I came to know through my work at the library: Tarla Mehta. Tarla had been born in Bombay and in her youth was an outstanding classical dancer – in fact it was said that Lord Mountbatten had once watched her dance, and later remarked that it was the most beautiful dancing he had ever seen. As is the case with many friendships, I can't pinpoint exactly when or how it started – it was as if I had always known her. One landmark, however, does stand out in my memory.

A Sikh girl named Sonia Singh, who worked in our Lending Department, was leaving to get married and we organised a celebratory meal for her at a local restaurant. That evening I was feeling very dejected, battered by recent events, and in no mood for celebration. Fortunately I had the good luck to sit beside Tarla. She started reminiscing about her life in India, and in particular told me some stories of a family pilgrimage to the Himalayas to worship the gods. By the end of the evening my mood was completely transformed. Those who can do this for a fellow human being are indeed very precious.

I also got to know Tarla's family: her handsome, intelligent husband Rajen, who worked as an adviser to the textile industry, and their two children Amru and Amrish. The children had inherited their parents' gifts: Amru was a scientist, but under her mother's guidance she had become a very fine dancer; Amrish was still at school, but he was already producing some interesting writings. In the company of this delightful family I went to many Indian cultural events, including dancing, music and religious ceremonies at the Hindu Temple.

When I think of that rich Indian artistic life transported into the alien setting of Huddersfield, music and dancing are at the fore. But Hindu culture also had one outstanding figure in the visual arts: Shanti Dutta. I only got to know Shanti on a fairly superficial level during what proved to be the last period of his life. Although only three years older than myself, he already had something of the look of an ancient guru, with his dark penetrating eyes and bushy beard.

Shanti had been born at Peshawar in 1933 in pre-partition India. Early on he showed an aptitude for art, and this led to six years at the College of Arts in New Delhi. The next bit of his life-story is quite romantic. While teaching art, he had as one of his pupils a young Sikh girl named Hermant, and they fell in love. Shanti was a Hindu, and furthermore a Brahmin. There were obviously going to be problems, especially as both of them already had arranged marriages lined up. There followed some years of separation: Shanti went to Prague in Czechoslovakia to study ceramics, and Hermant came to England and took up teaching in Huddersfield, where eventually they met again. She wrote to her father, and to their great relief he gave his blessing to their marriage. Thus, at long last, the wedding took place.

Many strands went into Shanti's work, including western influences such as cubism. As a rather wide generalisation it can be said that his earlier work was more abstract, and he later modulated to a mainly figurative approach, drawing largely on the mythology of Hinduism. *Blue Maiden* may be taken as an example of his early manner. It celebrates the eternal forces of renewal, both in the natural world and in human life. The girl is as yet inexperienced, the wine untouched, the casket unopened. Faint ripples stir on the yellow pond and the sea-green ocean. The eye in the rust-red mask looks out on the uncertain future, on its perils but also on its possibilities. But the leaves are already budding, and the blue maiden is waiting to inherit everything. If she stands firm, all these treasures will be hers.

Shanti was a man of wide enthusiasms, and even in the visual arts he tried many things – not just painting, but also ceramics, murals and batik. These activities influenced one another. Some of his paintings may make one think of ceramics, and he once did a series of pictures deliberately echoing the appearance of a row of tiles. His colours were always vibrant and his paintings full of vitality. But Shanti's impact on the community was not confined to his work as an artist. He was fond of music, and apparently had a fine voice, though I never heard him sing. Religion was also important to him, but not in a parochial or narrow-minded way. He was much involved with the Kirklees and Calderdale Interfaith Fellowship, in which people of different faiths came together and tried to understand one another's viewpoint. He was also active in promoting exhibitions of the work of other Indian artists as part of an effort to make their achievements better known in the west.

Sadly Shanti died in 1985, while still in his early 50s. So greatly was he esteemed that his body was taken to several of the widely differing places of religious worship before cremation. His great friend Anthony Mellor later wrote: 'When Shanti died so unexpectedly, I felt a deep sadness and a great personal loss.'

In January 1987, two years after Shanti's death, a retrospective exhibition of his work was held at Huddersfield Sports Centre. I was closely involved with this in my capacity as Secretary of Kirklees Arts Council. I vividly remember the opening. As the girls prepared the wine table, Tarla and Amru Mehta arrived, Tarla in pink and Amru in parrot green. Dr Nasim Hasnie, a prominent member of the Islamic community, gave the opening speech and then it was time for Amru to do her dances. I reminded the audience that these were religious dances, and asked them to refrain from smoking or drinking while they were in progress. Then Amru stepped forward and made a 'namaste' greeting, a slight bow with her hands together. She performed three dances, explaining each one beforehand. The beauty and grace of Indian classical dancing cannot be described in words; it has to be seen. Each movement is part of a story, and even a slight gesture with the hand may be significant. All the time Amru was dancing, her mother watched critically, and at the end of each dance Tarla would make a characteristic sign, just lifting a finger into the air as much as to say 'bravo'. The third dance told the famous story of Krishna as a very young boy running off with the milkmaids' clothes while they were bathing. I later wrote in my journal:

> Amru looked exquisitely beautiful in her costume of parrot green – with bangles and jewellery which jangled as she moved. Every pose and silhouette was lovely – her hands and eyes playing a vital part. There can be few more wonderful things than to watch an Indian girl dancing. Felt as I looked at her that I was getting an intangible insight into something deeply spiritual.

In the company of the Mehta family I also attended events celebrating the two great religious festivals in the Hindu calendar: Janamastami (the birth of Krishna), and Diwali (the return of Rama and Sita from the forest). Dwali is sometimes thought of as the nearest approach to Christmas. The ex-patriots in Huddersfield would reminisce about how they had celebrated it in India: the sending of cards, exchanging of gifts, the children letting off fireworks, and above all welcoming the Goddess Laxmi to their homes with marigold garlands over the door and designs drawn on the doorsteps.

   In the Yorkshire setting things were more subdued. A few close friends would be invited round for a meal, while at the Hindu Temple there would be a complete and continuous reading of the Tulsi Das version of the epic poem *The Ramayana*.* One year, however, the Hindu community opened its doors and let us all share in the celebrations by staging a pageant in the Town Hall. Anyone could come to this: Sikhs, Muslims, Ukrainians, West Indians, even Englishmen. To make the whole thing intelligible to all, Dr Tobarak Hossain would raise his dapper little figure above the stage every so often, and give a linking commentary. Thus we heard how Rávana the king of the demons had gained great power, because Brahma, impressed by Rávana's show of holiness, had promised that he would never be slain by god, demon, spirit or serpent. Only a man could kill him, but Rávana wasn't worried about that, for he despised man. So he wrought great evil on Earth: he destroyed the gods' pleasure gardens; carried off nymphs and celestial dancers; and scattered the sacrifices of the blessed hermits. Brahma and the other gods decided that only by one of them entering into a man could Rávana be destroyed, and so Vishnu entered part of his spirit into the bodies of four brothers, the sons of King Dashrath: Rama, Bhárata, Shátrughna and Lákshmana.

---

* The original poem was composed by Valmiki in the fourth century BC but not written down in Sanskrit until the sixth century AD. The sixteenth-century Tulsi Das version is in Hindi.

Amru Mehta dancing at the opening of the Shanti Dutta retrospective exhibition, Huddersfield Sports Centre, 23 January 1987. (Courtesy of the Huddersfield Examiner)

The first scene – the court of King Dashrath – appeared on the wide Town Hall stage. He stood at the centre, old, grey-bearded and wearing a doti of gold. Around him was his entourage – three queens, four sons, the sons' wives and their servants, amid a great shimmering of crowns and saris. With their strange dark eyes and dark faces, they were glowing and handsome.

And so throughout the long evening the great drama of the Ramayana was unfolded. In the intervals we ate exotic food and chatted among ourselves. Then Dr Hossain's sonorous voice would declaim the next development of the story, until we came to the final scene: Rama and Sita, the eternal male and female, returned from their long exile in the forest to reclaim the kingdom that was rightfully theirs.

However, I think my most vivid memory of Hindu cultural events is of the celebration of Janamastami (the birth of Krishna) at the Hindu Temple in Zetland Street. Coincidentally it was also the last time I saw Shanti Dutta. I went there with the Mehta family and my 17-year-old daughter Beth. Zetland Street, short though it was, certainly contained paradoxes. The Zetland pub itself was well known to me as the meeting place of Kirklees Poetry Society, and its landlady, Mrs Allen, was once the tap-dance champion of all England. The street also contained the Classic Cinema, the Irish Club, the Welfare Centre, the La Scala Italian Restaurant, and of course the Hindu Temple itself, which was really just an ordinary Huddersfield house that had been converted.

It was the first visit for both Beth and me, so we entered the place with excitement and trepidation, fearful of doing something wrong. We came into the hallway, took off our shoes and placed them in a rack. The well-carpeted stairs led us up to quite a spacious room. Pictures of divinities round the walls were garlanded with tinsel, and bells hung from the ceiling. The floor had coloured chadars across the carpets for sitting on. At the end furthest from the window there were some Alhambra-type arches, and beyond these on the stage stood the smiling statuettes of the gods: Hanuman – the monkey god; Ganesh – the elephant-headed god; Rama and Sita – the eternal male and female; Vishnu – all cobalt-blue; and of course Krishna himself – the cheeky boy who was also a sage and a god.

We went towards the stage and made our donations of fruit, flowers and money, while Tarla and Rajen made a pranam gesture of reverence. The chanting had already started. Near the stage an oldish woman in a blue sari sang a line, and the 'congregation' sitting cross-legged on the floor responded, with all the pieces enshrining the many legends of Krishna. We sat down. Males were supposed to sit on one side, females on the other – but the borderline was very haphazard, and Beth was actually sitting beside me. Small children wandered everywhere.

At this early stage there were relatively few people around. The whole thing warmed up slowly, like a long crescendo. After about an hour we went downstairs for some tea. There seemed to be more people here than upstairs. We sat at a table and a very sick-looking man brought us tea, channas and jhalebi. We were a very mixed bunch. Shanti Dutta was there, as was the priest, wearing a yellow 'waistcoat', and with a band of yellow dye running vertically down his forehead. By my side sat a local bus driver, an Indian with a strong Yorkshire accent. He told us he had lived in Huddersfield for thirty years, but this was his first visit to the Temple. 'I were walking past a few weeks ago, and somehow just seeing Temple brought things back – back from when I were a kid in India – lovely colourful memories. And I said to myself: "At Janamastami I go in – revive all them wonderful memories."'

We went back upstairs to discover that the proper ceremony was only just starting; all the previous activity had been but a warming-up session. Shanti stood up and gave a brief introduction in English. He then came and sat just in front of me. The priest then addressed the room, but as he spoke in Hindi I couldn't understand a word. The chanting resumed, the rest of us responding to the principal singer either vocally, by clapping or by playing a musical instrument. Various instruments were distributed to the gathering, mostly pairs of cymbals about 2in across and small elongated drums. I found myself landed with a chimta, a steel strip with jingling discs attached. After I had made a few very inept attempts to play the thing, Shanti kindly took it from me, showed me the correct method of playing it and handed it back. Most of the singing was very lively but then a very small pretty girl in pink with long dark hair reaching to the floor began to chant, and everyone else fell silent. (I learnt later that she was from south India, and no one knew her song or the legend it enshrined.) A local doctor broke the subdued atmosphere with his deep resonant voice, and then Tarla sang the song about Krishna and the milkmaids. Everyone knew this one and joined in.

As midnight approached, the time when the infant god was to be born into this world, things built to a climax: the joss-sticks wafted their scent across the room; the tinsel flashed back light from the walls; the gods and goddesses beamed down at us. (Beth leant across and whispered in my ear: 'Can you believe that this is really happening?') Rose petals were passed among the women and holy water was splashed across the room. A girl went round ladling panchamrit into our cupped hands. Trays with small lighted candles were circulated, and we held our hands above the flames and then spread the warmth across our faces.

Midnight came. Briefly the lights went out, and all we could see were the candles burning in front of Rama and Sita. Then the lights went on again, and everyone stood up. This was the moment of Krishna's birth. We all moved forward; bells were rung, gongs sounded and there was a great blast from a conch shell. Then one by one we rocked the infant god in his cradle. It was the most truly spiritual experience of my life.

Suddenly it was all over. We went downstairs, put on our shoes and went out of the front door. And there we were back in Zetland Street: a drunk coming out of the Irish Club; the clatter of plates in the La Scala Restaurant; the stars in the cold Yorkshire sky.

Bright sari in a darkened street –
the lilting grey of Yorkshire sky;
rust requiems for demolished mills –
repeating grooves of curlew's cry.

And did Jane once sit on this stile
to watch the moon look down on Hay,
and see the dog and hear the horse
send icy clatters through the grey?

Then later – only you to wait
(dogs rush to greet the friends not there)
the bloodstains of the sunset sink –
the red Decembers of despair.

And worlds still pirouette their stars,
while on that stage fresh actors meet,
dim picture in a golden frame –
bright sari in a darkened street.

11

A Daughter and a Dog

The mention of my daughter in the previous chapter brings me back to the little happenings of my own personal life, which I have somewhat lost track of in these cultural meanderings. The days at the library went by with their curious mixture of pleasure and irritating trivia. And my more intimate life was by no means uneventful. Relationships came and went, a few of them transforming into lasting friendships.

In the midst of the chaotic muddle that constitutes most of life, I always find something reassuring about the perpetual rhythm of the seasons. All have an equal beauty in my opinion, although spring seems to be most people's favourite, and the poets have certainly devoted more verses to it than any other. Certainly there is something magical about an apparently dull day towards the end of winter: the distant Pennines are still deep in snow, and everything has a subdued air of dormancy, but suddenly a single ray of sunlight illuminates a sycamore, and you notice that it is finally in bud. Soon the springtime gorse blooms along the heights, and the woods at Ellen Springs are full of bluebells. The water from the melting snow would leave fields and paddocks covered in mud and puddles, but this wouldn't prevent small girls on fat little ponies from galloping around and churning up the ground.

At the library the purple-bound copies of Maunder's *Olivet to Calvary* and Stainer's *Crucifixion* would be issued to the less ambitious choirs. (I remember a story of a choirmaster being asked what he thought of Stainer's *Crucifixion*, and replying that he was all for it!) I preferred more substantial fare to get me into the Easter mood, and would borrow the record set of Bach's *St Matthew Passion*, listening to a side every morning at breakfast. Easter is a movable feast, but it usually coincided with the daffodils alongside the church path reaching their full glory, while my own garden flourished with chionodoxas, scilla sibiricas and the last of the winter-flowering heathers.

On 15 May one year I wrote in my journal:

9.45 a.m. – a lovely warm sunny morning – without a cloud. House-martins flying around – swooping down and clinging briefly to the wall beneath the eaves – reconnoitring for a place to build a nest. Pond swarming with tadpoles. Robert next door (now aged one and a half) playing with his building bricks in the sunshine.

Those birds, the house-martins and swallows, seem the very signature tune of summer – their coming marking its start and their departure the season's ending. Often at Thurstonland we would see the first swallows about the time of the local elections, with the earliest of the tribe swooping above us as we went in to vote at the village school, which served as a polling station. Whatever broken promises we might fear from the politicians, the return of the swallows was always reassuring.

Another vivid memory of the Thurstonland summer is of the evening sunlight shining on the whites of the cricketers, as their games stretched on into the long light evening hours. By then the meadow crane's bill would be in bloom on the lower slopes of Pike Stye, and in the neglected corners of the churchyard the inflorescences of rosebay willow herb mimicked the shape of the tower beyond. For me these beautiful magenta flowers always bear a message of hopefulness. This is partly because I can remember seeing them blossom on London's bombsites after the terrible devastation of the Second World War, and partly because they are at the best in late July, the time of my birthday.

Round about early September the swallows and house-martins would become singularly voluble, chattering away beneath the eaves of the Village Hall. 'Oh yes – they hold meetings,' Amy Jackson the caretaker informed me. What exactly was discussed one could only guess, but sure enough, about a fortnight later they were off to warmer climes. Sometimes the migration seemed quite abrupt. 'The swallows left on Thursday,' Mrs Holmes once told me when I returned from a visit to Ireland, and had phoned her to reorder the milk. Yet strangely enough there were usually a few stragglers. Some while afterwards one would spot a sprinkling of birds still playing in the air above the village roofs, as if they were reluctant to set off on the great trek.

Another phenomenon I associate with autumn at Thurstonland is the blooming of a patch of Michaelmas daisies to the south of the road over the Heights. Michaelmas daisies in gardens were one thing, but why should they grow out here in the wild? Even more intriguing was the adjoining area that was covered with pale mauve flowers. I spent ages poring over Keble Martin's *Concise British Flora* trying to identify them, but it was my horticultural friend John Cutter who pinned them down: soapwort (otherwise known as Bouncing Bet), but not the wild form – a cultivated one. There are many spots in the countryside like this. No doubt long ago a cottage had stood at the spot. Every stone of it has now vanished, but every year up come the soapworts and the Michaelmas daisies, the last vestiges of a once carefully tended garden.

The rest that I remember of the season is what everybody knows: the lifting of the potatoes on Farnley Moor, the building of the Guy Fawkes bonfire on the recreation ground, and the gold and russets of the beeches and sycamores in Brown's Knoll Wood.

For some the cold days of winter with their late dawns and early dusks are a time of melancholy, even depression. I never feel like that, being a sufferer from MWC (Mid-Winter Cheerfulness). So far as I know (and hope) the complaint is incurable. On a crisp morning when the night-fallen snow has frozen on the branches, when the sky is blue, and even the wettest pathways are firmed by frost and easily passable

– on such a morning cheerfulness is pardonable. But even on dull wet days, when the hills are all blotted out by drizzling sleet, and the robins and blue-tits crowd around the bird table – for me at least, there is still a certain indefinable charm.

At Thurstonland I heard stories of various past winters. During the famous snowfalls of early 1947 legend had it that the drifts were so deep you could walk over hedges and walls without realising they were there! The worst I experienced was in early 1979, and I remember the snow-shifters working frantically in Marsh Hall Lane. On such mornings I would put on my boots, walk down Thurstonland Bank and try to hitch a lift on the main road – and I always got to work, somehow.

At the library, too, winter would have its particular pattern and characteristics. In the weeks before Christmas there would be a great demand for Christmassy records, not just carols but also such works as Charpentier's *Midnight Mass for Christmas Eve*, *The Childhood of Christ* by Berlioz and Bach's *Christmas Oratorio*. There were in fact some musical events which were unique to the area; certain ancient carols for example were only sung in the vicinity of Meltham.* But of course the events which everyone knows about are the annual performances of *Messiah*. I remember my old friend Malcolm Cruise, whom I had known in the army, and who had gone on to better things as the music critic for the *Huddersfield Examiner*, coming into the library about mid-December. In answer to my enquiry as to how he was getting on, he replied: 'Three down and three to go.' For better or worse, *Messiah* has become an institution, as difficult to judge objectively as a work of art as Nelson's Column is as a work of sculpture. The queues for the Huddersfield Choral Society's public performance would stretch right round the Town Hall. After five years' residence I became a member. And thus we went through the great ritual: the singing of 'Christians Awake' beforehand; the tenor's opening words 'Comfort ye, comfort ye, my people' (after all the shuffling around for seats, one was in need of a bit of comfort); the standing up for the 'Hallelujah Chorus' in the George II tradition (whoever said the monarchy didn't have influence); and finally that wonderful high note for the sopranos in the closing bars of the 'Amen Chorus' – which even now always thrills me. But for those a bit weary of all this it can be a salutary experience to sit back in the restfulness of one's own living room, and hear the beauty of the work speak for itself. My fellow poet Stephen Henderson Smith once wrote to the *Huddersfield Examiner* suggesting that these annual performances of *Messiah* should be given a rest for a bit, and some other work substituted. Needless to say, his suggestion was not implemented. I think the streets of Huddersfield would have been running with blood if it had!

Into this world of alien culture, of the small hilltop village and the Yorkshire town, walked my 16-year-old daughter Beth. For most of her life she had lived in that area of sprawling suburbia where London merges slowly into the Surrey countryside.

* A record of these was produced many years ago by the Melvo Singers.

Beth at Haworth. (Author's collection)

Finding herself among the woods and fields was a great novelty, although the first place she wanted to visit was the Beatles Museum in Liverpool. On the train back we read to each other from the Merseybeat poets. A bit later we went to Malham, and she was enthralled by the towering rocks of Gordale Scar. The circular walk round Gordale, the Tarn and the Cove became very special to her. A local popular route was round Brown's Knoll Wood and the switchback; in fact we christened this walk 'Beth's Favourite'.

The sudden appearance of a 16-year-old girl at my home was bound to cause comment. A certain lady in the village remarked to Constance Adamson that

'Mr Emberson's new girlfriend is far too young for him', and it had to be explained to her that Beth was my daughter.

There were various ups and downs, as there are bound to be when two people have to adjust to living together. Beth's earlier life had been somewhat restricted, and I think she both relished and feared her new-found freedom. At parties, dances and night-clubs she just wasn't quite sure how to behave. But little by little she relaxed. For the first two years she was studying at sixth-form college and soon made friends. She would invite them up to our home at Thurstonland, and I got involved in a world of youth culture which was new to me. I drew on something of this in my novel *Kavita*, which was written about this time, but it also owed much to the Indian traditions I had encountered through Tarla and her family.

After leaving college Beth had a succession of jobs in a short space of time, at the Famous Army Stores and various pubs, and for quite some while she was a barmaid at Johnny's nightclub (an unlikely career move for someone who had signed the pledge!). I remember at one time there was a Spanish fellow named Jesus working as a cook in the establishment – and to me the idea of the second coming occurring at Johnny's nightclub seemed rather incongruous!

Beth with her records. (Author's collection)

After a while Beth inherited some money from my Aunt Jessie, and she bought herself a small cottage at Slant Gate, Cowlersley, at the edge of the Colne Valley. Now that we were no longer living cheek by jowl we got on better, although at the same time she was within easy reach, so I spent a lot of time at Slant Gate and she likewise at Thurstonland.

Beth was an attractive girl and there were always boys hovering around, and I found myself being drawn into these relationships in various ways. One relationship in particular was destined to make a considerable impact on my life. The boy's mother had a heart attack, and was rushed to hospital. My contribution to the crisis was to take her mongrel bitch Goldie into my home and look after her. To complicate matters Goldie was pregnant – indeed, the evening she came into my place I was informed she might give birth that very night. However, I was determined to do my bit to help, even though at this stage I wouldn't have considered myself a dog lover. But as soon as Goldie walked through the door I knew we would get on well. It was already dark, but we went for a short walk together. Next morning I came downstairs feeling a bit apprehensive as to what I might find. But no, all was well – she hadn't given birth. It was a sunny morning and later on I took her for a walk in Matthewman's Woods, and suddenly found what a wonderful companion a dog can be. At this time I was just completing the first draft of *Kavita*, and would write a few pages at the kitchen table immediately after breakfast. Goldie would curl up at my feet, and I felt her presence as a comfort and inspiration.

Thus a week passed. On the Saturday I took Goldie for her morning's walk along Occupation Lane, and noticed she was trembling slightly. When I got home she immediately lay down in her basket. After a bit I observed what I took to be a piece of black rag. Then I saw that it seemed to be moving of its own volition, and realised it was a puppy's tail. Two more puppies were born, then Goldie went out to the back garden for a wee, before returning to her basket to give birth to three more, all in a very matter-of-fact sort of way, without fuss or emotion. There was actually a seventh puppy, but it was born dead and Goldie ate it. I was rather alarmed at this, but I gather from people better informed in canine matters that this is quite common. The first born was pure black, and the last born pure white; these two were males; the intervening four were various combinations of brown and white, and all females.

For a month Goldie lay at my feet as I wrote, and accompanied me on my walks while the puppies cavorted around the living room. Then one morning she and the puppies went back to their owner. I wasn't prepared for the terrible sense of emptiness which their going created, and went for a walk to pull myself together. I remember that as I approached Shepley Wood End Farm I heard a dog barking in the distance, and had to deviate from the footpath. In that frame of mind I couldn't bear to see a dog belonging to someone else.

However, my dogless state didn't last long. Five puppies all found good homes elsewhere but Beth had had an especial affection for the first-born, whom we had christened Sooty, and he went to live with her at Slant Gate. Occasionally I would 'borrow' him and take him for walks, and even at this early stage I could sense a

Beth and Sooty near Stoodley Pike. (Author's collection)

strong bond between us. Eventually Beth won a place at Bangor University to study mathematics, and Sooty came to live with me.

It was on an afternoon in early January that Sooty (now nearly 3 years old) returned to the house of his birth. Almost immediately we set off on a walk together. It was already mid-afternoon when I parked the car near Ramsden Reservoir. Then we climbed up through the conifers, across to Holme Styles Reservoir, past the two curiously named ruined farms, Elysium and Hades, along Barebones Road and finally back to the car, by which time the sunset had faded and the half-moon was already shining brightly. When we got home Sooty was far too weary to do anything but curl up in his basket and sleep. Next morning I did my usual morning's writing with Sooty at my feet, and discovered, as with Goldie, the

Sooty and his sister Whiskey at the Honley Show. (Courtesy of the Huddersfield Examiner)

exquisite pleasure of an animal's presence. I noted in my journal that, curiously enough, I found it easier to concentrate in the company of a dog.

Sooty, like every animal, had his own idiosyncratic character, his own especial likes and dislikes – often seemingly totally irrational. He hated to be left alone in the house. I only tried the experiment a few times, and he always showed his annoyance by some form of naughtiness. On one occasion he drank all the contents of a bottle of cooking oil, and then spewed it up on the carpet. That was the very last time I left him alone in the house. Conversely he seemed quite content to be left in the far more confined space of the car for hours on end. I found myself planning my days around his likes and dislikes.

I always took Sooty with me when I went into the countryside to do a painting. He seemed quite content to lie patiently by my side while the work progressed. At such times he was singularly protective, and would utter a low growl if anyone approached. Perhaps he thought he was guarding a masterpiece. How wrong he was!

There is always a problem when one wishes to paint a scene which is far from any highway. You can of course just put a sketch pad and a camera in the rucksack, do sketches and take photos on the spot, and then at a later date, in the comfort of your studio, base a painting on the sketches and photos. However, there is always something special about painting direct from the scene. One summer day I decided I would paint Top Withens near Haworth. The nearest I could get the car was Scar Top, close to Ponden Reservoir. From here I had to carry my equipment: my acrylic paints, the piece of hardboard with the watercolour paper attached, jar, water and brushes. There was also Sooty to keep an eye on. To make matters worse, it was excessively hot.

Eventually we reached the lonely ruined farmhouse with its two sycamores, surrounded by moorland. I was feeling almost too shattered to lift a paintbrush. Fortunately we were fairly free from interruptions; only a few sheep walked by indifferently. Then at the end of three hours' work there was the labour of returning to Scar Top. And the result of all this effort? A picture so utterly worthless that on returning home I ripped it up and threw it in the bin!

Haworth Parsonage in the snow. (Author's collection)

12

The Brontës

Top Withens is of course supposedly 'in that book what those Brontë people wrote about like' – as Arthur had helpfully informed us on the Pennine Way. The Brontës seem to have been tangled up in my life for a long time, since long before my move to Yorkshire. When I was still a child my mother acted as housekeeper to my Uncle Bill at his big house in Hertfordshire. In the dining room there was a very large sofa among other things, and we children regarded the gap between it and the wall as a sort of secret passage. At the end we came face to face with a massive bookcase, its front guarded by doors with metal scrolls and glass, and locked with a key that fortunately was never removed. Near the centre of the case were two books, *Wuthering Heights* (which was blue) and *Jane Eyre* (which was brown), the spines of which were decorated with a flaming torch, the symbol of the Classics Book Club. (The self-same copies are beside me as I write.) For some strange reason I was drawn to them, and when the adults were away I would unlock the bookcase, extract the precious volumes and look at the pictures. The one showing the mad-woman's visit to Jane Eyre's bedroom particularly fascinated me. The fact that these books had belonged to my uncle's long-dead first wife only added to their attraction.

Such premonitions in early childhood of things which will be important in adulthood are curious, but not uncommon. Our friend Pearl Cragg had a similar early experience with the Brontës. The first she can remember is sitting by the fire with her mother and hearing a radio programme about their lives. Somehow it fascinated her, particularly the fact that they had lost their mother. A short while later her father was going on a car journey across the north of England, his route taking him close to Haworth. Pearl sat on the back seat clutching a map, and every so often would make such remarks as 'only half an inch to Haworth'. When they reached the village it was evening. They parked at the bottom of Main Street, and Pearl ran up the cobbles to the Parsonage. Of course it was closed, but she touched the front gate and ran back to her parents. 'That will have to do for the time being,' she said. And this was the prelude to a life-long passion. Even now, as an elderly lady, she makes an annual pilgrimage to Haworth and stays at a guest-house, so that she can attend the Brontë Society events and be refreshed by the whole atmosphere of the place.

❖   ❖   ❖

Top Withens near Haworth, thought by some to be the original of 'Wuthering Heights', although the now-demolished High Sunderland Hall near Halifax had a better claim. (Author's collection)

If there is one moment in the lives of the Brontës when I would have liked to have been a proverbial fly on the wall it is the morning of 6 June 1826, when the four surviving children awoke to discover the box of wooden soldiers. The previous day their father had been to a theological gathering in Leeds, and while there had bought some toys for his children. He arrived home late, after the children had gone to bed. Three years later Charlotte wrote a description of what happened the following morning:

> Papa bought Branwell some wooden soldiers at Leeds; when Papa came home it was night and we were in bed, so next morning Branwell came to our door with a box of soldiers. Emily and I jumped out of bed, and I snatched up one and exclaimed, 'This is the Duke of Wellington! This shall be the Duke!' When I had said this Emily likewise took one up and said it should be hers; when Anne came down, she said one should be hers. Mine was the prettiest of the whole, and the tallest, and the most perfect in every part. Emily's was a grave-looking fellow, and we called him 'Gravey'. Anne's was a queer little thing, much like herself, and she called him 'Waiting boy'.* Branwell chose his and called him 'Bonaparte'.

* Emily and Anne's soldiers were later renamed after the polar explorers Sir William Parry (1790–1855) and Sir John Ross (1777–1856). There were in fact two polar explorers of the name of Ross – Sir John Ross and his nephew Sir James Clark Ross (1800–62). It is impossible to guess which of them the young Anne Brontë had in mind – possibly both.

Thus they began to 'weave a web in childhood'. At first their fantasies about the soldiers were simply played out, in the same way that many children act out their imaginary stories. Three years later Charlotte (then aged 13) wrote the description quoted above. But having described the origin of their imaginary world, the children went on to write out the actual stories themselves, in small books bound in sugar paper and using minute handwriting – as if the books were written by the toy soldiers they describe. After a while Emily and Anne broke away and created their own imaginary world of Gondal, a bleak island in the north Pacific, while Charlotte and Branwell continued to write the history of Angria, a country supposedly set close to present-day Nigeria. Despite its tropical position, Angria possessed heathery moors very similar to those of Yorkshire, and even Boulsworth Hill makes a brief appearance!

Charlotte and Branwell continued with these writings up until adulthood, and Anne until a few years before her death, but Emily carried on writing about Gondal (and Gaaldine, a warmer island in the south Pacific) until the end of her life. Her very last surviving piece is a Gondal poem written after *Wuthering Heights*. The

The Old Vicarage, Cross Stone, near Todmorden, where the 13-year-old Charlotte Brontë wrote her first surviving letter. It is about ten minutes' walk from the author's present home. (Author's collection)

prose writings connected with Gondal and Gaaldine have disappeared and we can only make tentative reconstructions of the storyline from the related poems. But most of Charlotte and Branwell's juvenilia has survived.

Those who haven't read these early writings cannot be aware what a remarkable body of literature they constitute. The sheer size is amazing. I once estimated that the combined juvenilia of Charlotte and Branwell (which in a sense comprises one gigantic novel) is equal in length to about one and a half times that of *War and Peace* – an incredible achievement for two young children. In some ways it's a gigantic novel, but in many respects it's more like a cross between an epic poem and a soap opera.* The four Genii, Brannii, Tallii, Emmii and Annii, look down protectively on their heroes, rather as the Greek gods looked down on Achilles and Odysseus. At the same time various characters hold the thread together without any overall plot, somewhat in the manner of *The Archers* or *Coronation Street*. Curious as this combination may seem, it offers endless possibilities for invention, and the juvenilia has certain dimensions that are lacking in the adult novels. There is almost a feeling that the characters exist in a parallel universe.

'Isolation' is a word much used by some authorities on the Brontës. Others, such as Juliet Barker, have stressed the exact opposite, pointing out their strong contacts with the world beyond Haworth. In a sense both are right. Through newspapers and periodicals the Brontë children had a knowledge of contemporary politics and society which would be unusual even today. But to some extent they created their own isolation, taking in all that they needed from the outside world and feeding it into their own world of the imagination.

The story of the Brontë children bears a striking resemblance to the histories of two other remarkable early nineteenth-century families, the Rossettis and the Mendelssohns. In each case there were four highly gifted siblings, some of them talented in more than one branch of the arts; they were all very close and shared their creativity. They also grew up within a somewhat alien culture.

The Mendelssohns were Jewish by birth, although the whole family later converted to the Lutheran Church. It is a little-known fact that the children suffered anti-Semitic abuse. The Rossettis were three-quarters Italian; only their maternal grandmother was English. There is something unmistakably Italian in the creations of Christina and Dante Gabriel. But they are also intensely English – read for example Christina's 'The Green Cornfield'. Somehow the two cultures have been blended in the creative world which the children shared, and they emerge as highly individual expressions of an ethos that is neither Italian nor English. Likewise the Brontës. They are usually thought of as Yorkshire writers – most of their more popular stories and poems have a Yorkshire setting. Yet they didn't have a drop of Yorkshire blood in their veins. Their father was Irish, born near Drumballyroney just west of the Mountains of Mourne in County Down, and their mother Maria (née Branwell) was from Penzance in Cornwall. Some of the strange elements in their writings can be partly explained by this Celtic background. I was once sitting in the

* I'm indebted to Bob Barnard for the soap opera idea.

Packhorse Bridge, Wycoller. This area is traditionally linked with the final chapters of Charlotte Bronte's Jane Eyre. *(Author's collection)*

Four Cousins café at Huddersfield, half-listening to the conversation of an Irish woman at an adjoining table. When she had gone I took out a volume of Emily Brontë's poems and started reading. After a bit I realised I was hearing them in my mind's ear with an Irish accent, and it seemed totally appropriate:

> Cold in the earth, and the deep snow piled above thee!
> Far, far removed, cold in the dreary grave!
> Have I forgot, my Only Love, to love thee,
> Severed at last by Time's all-wearing wave?

It was Emily's poetry that was to provide the catalyst for the sisters' last outpouring of shared creativity. As so often the story is told by Charlotte:

One day, in the autumn of 1845, I accidentally lighted on a MS volume of verse in my sister Emily's handwriting. Of course I was not surprised, knowing that she could and did write verse: I looked it over, and something more than surprise seized me – a deep conviction that these were not common effusions, nor at all like the poetry women generally write. I thought them condensed and terse, vigorous and genuine. To my ear, they had also a peculiar music – wild, melancholy and elevating. . . .*

* Charlotte Brontë, 'Biographical notice of Ellis and Acton Bell', see the preliminary material in Emily Brontë's *Wuthering Heights* edited with an introduction by Ian Jack, Oxford University Press, 1976.

The story of what that discovery led to has been often told: Emily's initial hostility; Charlotte somehow overcoming that hostility; Anne quietly producing some of her own poems. The upshot of all this was the publication in 1846 of *Poems by Currer, Ellis and Acton Bell*, these being the pseudonyms under which they veiled their identity. Two copies of the book were sold. It says much for their determination that, despite this rebuff, they went on to produce three 'prose tales': Charlotte wrote *The Professor*, Emily *Wuthering Heights* and Anne *Agnes Grey*. These started their rounds of the publishers, at first with the disappointing results which most authors are all too familiar with. Eventually, however, Newby accepted the works by Emily and Anne. Meanwhile, Charlotte, now in Manchester nursing her father after an eye operation, had started *Jane Eyre*. She wrote rapidly, and shortly after completion the book was accepted by Smith Elder and published in October 1847. Thus, although it was not the earliest written, *Jane Eyre* was the first Brontë novel to be published. *Wuthering Heights* and *Agnes Grey* followed three months later.

This second period of shared creativity was destined to last for only three years, from 1845 to 1848, during which time the sisters produced most of the writings for which they are best remembered. Compared with the shared creativity of their childhood, this second period had one important element missing: Branwell. A series of disasters had virtually destroyed his spirit, and he was now sunk in drink and drugs. In September 1848 he died, and his death was soon followed by those of Emily and Anne. Charlotte, left alone in the Parsonage with her father, wrote one more masterpiece, the wonderfully poignant *Villette*, before she too died in March 1855.

Much has been written about the works they left. I only want to add one small observation: that Haworth, the mecca of all Brontë enthusiasts, is scarcely ever depicted. True there are a few scattered references. In Charlotte's early story *My Angria and the Angrians*, Haworth and some of its inhabitants (notably the Brontë family themselves) are made fun of under the name of 'Howard'. Elsewhere in the juvenilia we get a delightful description of a cold winter's day in the village:

> . . . when the icicles are hanging from the eaves of the houses. . . . When all the old women traverse the streets in real woollen cloaks and clanking iron pattens. When apothecaries are seen rushing about with gargles and tinctures and washes for sprained ankles, chilblains and frost-bitten noses. When you can hardly feel your hands and feet for the cold and are forced to stand shuddering over the fire on pain of being petrified by the frost.*

Then there are the opening pages of *Agnes Grey* and a few of the poems by Anne and Emily, in particular Emily's expression of homesickness:

---

* Christine Alexander (ed.), *An Edition of the Early Writings of Charlotte Brontë*, vol. 1, Basil Blackwell for the Shakespeare Head Press, 1987, p. 118.

> The mute bird sitting on the stone,
> The dank moss dripping from the wall,
> The garden-walk with weeds o'er grown,
> I love them – how I love them all!*

It is curious that they so seldom depicted Haworth, for, despite strenuous efforts to ruin it, the place has a strong atmosphere. And it is an atmosphere that can only be glimpsed in a day's visit. One needs to linger over the place, walk the surrounding countryside, and to see Haworth itself in its various moods.

Every year I went over in early June for the cluster of events organised by the Brontë Society. Usually I would travel across each day from Thurstonland, but in June 1988 I decided to stay there. Though I could not know it at the time, those five days were destined to change the course of my life.

I put up at the Copper Kettle, a rather delightful establishment halfway up the steep slope of Main Street. Of the first five days I remember the events themselves in a somewhat secondary way. On the Friday there was a so-called Yorkshire Evening. This started off with an eating session: a meat pie capped with a dollop of mushy peas, plus parkin and shortbread, the whole washed down with plentiful cups of tea. (After a few days of this sort of thing I began to suspect that the Brontë Society was only a cover-up for a bunch of compulsive eaters.) Then Mary Woolridge, who ran the Parsonage Bookshop, gave a reading. She was dressed in period costume, and had that indefinable blessing – a 'Brontë'-type voice. Saturday brought the Church Service, the annual lecture, the AGM and a cheese and wine party. On the Sunday there was a concert in the church, and I remember Virginia Rushton's soprano voice sounding out wonderfully in the resonant acoustic. Afterwards I went to a party with some of the performers. Leaving somewhat late, I found myself locked out of the Copper Kettle and had to spend the night at a friend's.

However, all this has faded somewhat in my memory compared with the atmosphere of the place itself. The cobbled Main Street has its charms at every part of the day. In the bright sunlight of early morning it seems deserted, except for numerous tom-cats skulking in and out of ginnels, and a few hens pecking at morsels. Then the cleaner at the Fleece Inn appears periodically at the door to shake out a broom or a duster. Once the tourists arrive the street has the feel of a continuous festival: many tongues are heard and many strange garments seen, as people wend their way in and out of shops, pubs and cafés. There is such an air of conviviality that I would find myself talking to complete strangers in a manner utterly incompatible with normal English reserve. And then there is the late evening, when most of the tourists have gone home, a thin rain falls on the steep cobbles, and the old street-lamps shine murkily through the gloom. A solitary drunk slouches on a wall near the Black Bull shouting abuse – some Haworth traditions die hard.

* 'A little while, a little while . . .', *Emily Jane Brontë, The Complete Poems*, edited by Janet Gezari, Penguin, 1992, p. 88.

Most days I went into the countryside for a few hours: crossing the boggy Oxenhope Moor through the thin rain with curlews and lapwings crying around me, or climbing Crow Hill (the scene of the famous bog-burst of 1824). More memorable was the Sunday afternoon, when I took my art equipment to a spot on the hillside near Foster's Leap and did a painting in acrylics of the scene before me. In the foreground were the twisted hawthorns and vaccary walls, while below me in the valley lay the hamlet of Wycoller with its ancient bridges and ruined hall (perhaps the original of Ferndean Manor in *Jane Eyre*). Beyond the village were sloping fields and woods, a glimpse of Colne and Barrowford, and over all this the grey outline of Pendle Hill, like a cumbrous dog with its flattened head pressed to the ground. But more than all this I remember the sky: a great volume of cumulus cloud moving mass after mass across the zenith, the sunlight catching their bulging, gleaming peaks, their undersides all smouldering greyness, and amid the clouds occasional glimpses of clear sky, seeming incredibly blue.

On the Monday evening I went out with two postcards, intending to go no further than the post-box. But something led me on. It was a grey still evening; no sunshine, not a glimpse, yet it was wonderfully mild and inviting. As I left the village

The ruins of Wycoller Hall, possibly the Ferndean Manor of Jane Eyre. *From left to right: Catherine, Sooty and Siv Jansson.* (Author's collection)

Foster's Leap above Wycoller. (Author's collection)

a tawny owl was flying across the path on its silent mothy wings. A large flock of sheep was bleating down by the river, while from somewhere on the hillside above came the notes of the cuckoo, not just occasionally but continuously, the sound seeming to fill the valley. The air was quite windless and the reflections clear and perfect on the unruffled surface of Lower Laithe Reservoir. There were very few people around and I let my thoughts wander, feeling very much under the influence of the place. When I reached the spot sometimes known as the Meeting of the Waters I was completely alone. Unfortunately I found it was also the meeting place of the local gnats, and countless insects were love-dancing above the stream. So although I sat briefly in the Brontë Chair I felt less inclined to linger than I would otherwise. I went back to the village, and was lucky enough to see the tawny owl on the return journey also. The following day was to prove to be the most important of my life. . . .

13

Catherine

It is curious how trivial incidents can play a part in life's most important developments. This is particularly true of the start of relationships. One couple I know were brought together by failing to laugh at the same joke at a party. In my case, it all hinged on the fact that I had forgotten to take my water on a painting expedition. But here I am getting ahead of myself.

The train of events which I want to describe really started on the Sunday morning of that memorable stay at Haworth. A small party of us were taken on a conducted walk round the village, not just to the obvious places; some of the more obscure features were pointed out, such as the curious Celtic head at the end of West Lane. While on the walk I fell into conversation with Tony Holmes, a gentleman from Nottinghamshire, late middle-aged, moustached and handsome. He asked me where I came from. Normally I would have answered Huddersfield, but for some reason I said 'Thurstonland – it's a very small village – you won't have heard of it.' 'Not only have I heard of it,' Tony replied, 'but my father was born there – at Marsh Hall Farm.' This cemented our burgeoning friendship. I was introduced to his delightful wife Kay, and drew a sketch-map showing the position of Marsh Hall Farm in relation to my home, and invited them to visit me.

That afternoon I went on the painting expedition to Wycoller, described above. What I didn't mention before was that having reached the spot selected for its splendid view of Pendle Hill, I suddenly realised I'd forgotten the container of water which I always carry with me. There was nothing for it but to go back to the car for a small watering can, and descend to the stream to fill it. However, while so engaged I met Tony and Kay Holmes for the second time that day, and they in turn introduced me to their American friend Virginia Esson. She was to be another link in the chain.

Two days later, on the Tuesday, there was the annual Brontë Society coach excursion. This year it was to Gaskell Country – that is, the places around Manchester and Knutsford associated with Charlotte's friend and biographer Elizabeth Gaskell. Normally coach excursions are anathema to me, and I was very dubious about my chances of enjoying this one. On such events there is always the risk of finding oneself seated beside some terribly boring person, and having to put up with their company all day. In practice I found myself sitting alone, which didn't greatly please me either. However, the halt for 'elevenses' changed everything.

We stopped for coffee at the Gaskells' old home, 84 Plymouth Grove, Manchester. Being a great hater of coffee, I enquired after tea, but learnt that this

Catherine. (Photograph: Geoffrey Butterworth)

beverage was unobtainable. I then wandered into the drawing room, that famous apartment where most of the great literary figures of the nineteenth century had once held forth, including Dickens, Thackeray, Matthew Arnold and Ruskin – hopefully not looking as blank as I then felt. Fortunately Virginia Esson took pity on me, and taking me from the centre of the room led me to a secluded corner and introduced me to her two friends Pearl Cragg and Catherine Butterworth. Seating was limited, so I found myself kneeling on the carpet in front of these three ladies. Pearl and Virginia were middle-aged, but Catherine was younger, about 30 or so. While listening with a certain show of interest to Pearl telling us how much she was looking forward to meeting Charlotte Brontë in the afterlife, I was watching Catherine out of the corner of my eye. She had refined features, a clear but pale complexion, shortish dark brown hair, and a slim figure; she was not pretty, but was very definitely pleasing. I managed to draw her into the conversation. On being told her surname, I mentioned the composers George Butterworth and Arthur

Butterworth, but she had never heard of them. The talk then passed on to an article of hers about Stoodley Pike which had appeared in the Brontë Society *Transactions*. Pearl and Virginia had by now discreetly dropped out. I am not sure that elevenses is usually thought of as a romantic repast, but at the end of that one I knew I had met somebody very special.

The excursion continued with a visit to Mrs Gaskell's beautiful home town of Knutsford, with a meal at the Royal George and a guided tour of the town, topped off with a trip to the half-timbered Adlington Hall. By the end of the day I had got to know Catherine sufficiently well for an exchange of telephone numbers and addresses – essential items for the start of any relationship. I can remember sitting alone on the drive home (we were on separate coaches), and looking out across the flat Cheshire plain at the late evening sunlight just catching the curve of the great radio telescope at Jodrell Bank, and wondering when I would see that lovely girl again.

I need not have worried. That meeting on 7 June 1988 was the prelude to many meetings and partings as we oscillated between Catherine's home at Todmorden and mine at Thurstonland, about an hour's journey apart. As happens with many couples, the interest which originally linked us proved to be only one of a number of pursuits we had in common. We discovered, for example, that we both practised calligraphy. In the literary sphere there were many authors we both liked, and others we wished to explore. This led to our reading books together, and discussing them as we went along. Later, thanks to John Millington Synge, we started reading plays while sitting on the sofa. This worked fine if male and female characters were balanced evenly. If not, I had to adopt a high-pitched voice for the females and Catherine a low one for the males. When it came to music, Catherine's tastes were definitely on the lighter side, but we overlapped as far as Mozart was concerned. Of course there were things we didn't share. In the visual arts Catherine has a great passion for Van Gogh, which I can't enter into. Likewise I adore Gauguin, an artist she dislikes intensely. Our disagreement over these two rivals the eventual hostility of the men themselves.

Needless to say, no love relationship is entirely composed of love. As with all couples there were problems, differences and tiffs. (We even had a altercation over the spelling of tiffs – is it tifts or tiffs?) Oddly, the most serious arguments always seemed to spring from the most trivial causes. I remember one particularly vicious row over the best way to gather up hedge-clippings. Another, equally acute, arose out of a misunderstanding while we were making blackberry and apple jam. Catherine's instruction 'to put the pan on' meant merely that I should rest it on top of the cooker, but I interpreted it as meaning I should turn on the gas full blast. My usual reaction to these situations was to go for a brisk walk until the feeling of hostility on both sides had subsided. Sooty would, I think, prick up his ears hopefully at the commencement of any argument, and could hardly believe his luck as I hastily attached his lead and we strode off on a totally unexpected walk. But enough of quarrels – let us pass on to the pleasanter things. Three shared experiences must represent many others.

Norton Conyers, a spacious manor house built in the Dutch style, is situated in the countryside north of Ripon. Its main claim to fame is that it is usually thought of as the original of Thornfield Hall in *Jane Eyre*, the link being first established by Charlotte Brontë's great friend Ellen Nussey. There are other claimants to the title, including Ellen's old home at Rydings. However, Norton Conyers seems to tally in most points (though not all) with the description given in chapter 11 of the novel: 'It was three stories high, of proportions not vast though considerable: a gentleman's manor-house, not a nobleman's seat. . . .'

We visited Norton Conyers on a warmish day towards the end of August. The house is so shrouded in trees that there is no distant view of it from the main approach. I found myself abruptly driving up to the main doorway, and actually parked there for a few minutes. Then Catherine pointed out that this was a privilege reserved only for the lord of the manor, and indicated a car park a bit beyond that was more suited to plebs like myself.

We immediately felt the very tangible atmosphere of the place, something that is difficult to describe. The main front has an impressive doorway, and above are the four curvaceous gable-ends which give the house its Dutch-style appearance. A short distance in front of it runs a ha-ha (the 'sunken fence' of *Jane Eyre*), beyond which lies an area of parkland used for grazing sheep, with wide areas of grass and some fine old trees. Beyond this was more woodland, and then a distant view of the Pennines, all bluey-grey in the late summer heat.

We started off by looking round the walled garden, where there were some very unusual plants. Catherine kept asking me what they were, but despite my years in horticulture I was embarrassed to admit I didn't know them. There were also more familiar things, including blackberries, raspberries and apples, all in full fruit. A buddleia in purple bloom was covered in butterflies, peacocks, tortoiseshells and red admirals, as well as the more humble cabbage white. There was something about the place which made us think not so much of *Jane Eyre* as of Frances Hodgson Burnett's *The Secret Garden*.

The house itself was large, but without being one of those awful stately homes. One felt the sense of past generations.* Naturally Catherine and I were primarily interested in the Brontë connection, and were especially anxious to see the attic room where 'Mad Mary' was imprisoned – the episode which apparently gave Charlotte the idea for the first Mrs Rochester.

To begin we explored the main body of the house, starting with the entrance hall and its uninspiring family portraits. Things improved as we ascended the wide oak staircase, and saw the family group of Charles I's children. Admittedly it's only a copy, but a copy of a Van Dyck nevertheless. How confidently that young boy – the Prince of Wales and future Charles II – stands beside his enormous dog. We then inspected sundry four-poster beds, lesser pictures and wedding dresses, but we found no sign of an attic or Mad Mary's Room. Fortunately we fell into conversation with a very aristocratic lady attendant, and mentioned our especial interest. She explained

* See Sir James Graham, *A Guide to Norton Conyers*.

that the attic wasn't generally open to the public because the floor was unsafe. However, as we were so keen, she agreed after some hesitation to organise 'a tour'. She then muttered something about having 'lost old Sidney', and disappeared behind the scenes for a few minutes.

After a bit she re-emerged in the company of an oldish, rather ruinated-looking man, shabbily dressed and carrying a walking stick. This was 'old Sidney' Wright, who was destined to be our guide to the mysteries of the Norton Conyers attic.

We went through a side door and along a corridor. At the end Sidney abandoned his walking stick and we ascended a narrow, creaking staircase. The walls were covered with small pictures of nineteenth-century statesmen on horseback. At intervals there were landings and side-rooms. Each one was pointed out as 'the butler's room', 'the lady's maids' room' and so on. Every one was crammed with junk: screens, bedsteads, candle-holders, faded photographs behind smashed glass, third-rate paintings, fourth-rate copies and miscellaneous paraphernalia. There were two copies of a singularly awful painting showing a child with a hideously large head clutching a dove. We saw so much that I began to think old Sidney had forgotten all about 'Mad Mary's Room'. But oh no: 'We're coming to that.'

Eventually we came to the attic proper, low-roofed and dingy, and with the more dubious parts of the cement floor being covered with planks. In places the timbers were exposed, having been recently treated with a preservative. At the far end was 'Mad Mary's Room'. It is very plain and measures something like 15ft by 10ft. At the far end is one of the seven-paned windows which are a feature of Norton Conyers. Old Sidney said he could get no particular atmosphere from the room, but Catherine and I certainly felt we could.

So that was the end of 'the tour', and we returned via the winding staircase. Once back on the ground floor we were allowed a glimpse of the kitchen, its central arch festooned with everlasting flowers.

My second scene will be a brief one, but I know it will mean a lot to Catherine. It is a May morning above Bempton Cliffs near Flamborough Head, where the undulating Yorkshire Wolds end abruptly in 500ft-high chalk cliffs. Looking east there is in the distance a hint of sea-mist, but most of the sky is clear and blue, with long horizontal streaks of white cloud. At the edge of the cliffs pink campion blooms in profusion. And then there are the birds, seeming to assail us through every sense we possess. As we look down towards the calm sea, they are there in their thousands – flying, wheeling, turning, soaring, diving – and there is a great continuous screaming and crying. Only little by little do the individual species emerge. Kittiwakes predominate, true sea birds, who disdain to come inland and feed on rubbish dumps. Their gleaming white bodies and grey wings flashed back the morning sunlight, their 'kitti-way-ake' cry blending with the mêlée. The big herring gulls were less numerous. Along the ledges far below nested the guillemots and razorbills, both black and white, but the former somewhat larger, and the latter

Catherine and Sooty on Reddyshore Scout, near Todmorden. (Author's collection)

identifiable by its distinctive bill. They continuously quarrelled over space. How it is in the midst of all this chaos that they prevent their eggs from rolling into the sea I can't imagine – but the eggs are specially shaped to avoid rolling.

In the morning we walked east to a spot known as Staple Newk. Here there is a natural arch, and beyond it a small peninsula. This seemed to be the especial

Gannets on Bempton Cliffs. (Photograph: John Richardson)

preserve of the gannets, and they had commandeered every square inch of the chalky headland. Looking down from far above it is difficult to get a sense of scale, but they are in fact our biggest sea-birds, with a wingspan of up to 6ft. We watched them diving out at sea. They have no external nostril, and can hit the surface at 60mph without mishap.

In the afternoon we walked west to Jubilee Corner, and nearby experienced the climax of the day – the sight of a couple of puffins. Surely these are the cutest of birds, strangely comical, with the brilliant pinkish red of their feet and bill as their crowning glory.

Finally, back inland to the Calder Valley, and a warm July evening. For some while before my birthday I had had mysterious hints from Catherine that some sort of treat was in the offing. There was even a suggestion that we might be taken up in a hot-air balloon by a Todmorden group called 'The Bride's Nightie' – but knowing Catherine's fear of heights I thought this extremely improbable. However, it wasn't until we were driving to Hebden Bridge that she revealed that the treat consisted of a 'sunset supper cruise' aboard the canal barge *Sarah Siddons*. The day had been hot, and the early evening was still warm. Doors stood open in the terraced houses. Children played in the gardens, while their parents sat in deck-chairs sunning themselves. We arrived at the Hebden Bridge Marina to find a large brown carthorse with a white blaze munching hay, and the *Sarah Siddons*, its sides painted with roses and castles, moored alongside. We went aboard and took our seats on one of the benches that ran along both sides.

The captain appeared, dressed for the part in bowler hat, waistcoat, scarlet neckerchief, black trousers and clogs. 'Mr and Mrs Butterworth,' he shouted. It was a few moments before we realised he was referring to us – but it was just to check who was having the vegetarian meal. He then made a speech of welcome, informed us of the drill in the event of the vessel sinking (which seemed highly unlikely), and told us something of the history of the Rochdale Canal.* In addition to the captain, there appeared to be two members of crew, along with Emma, the very charming young barmaid, Max the horse (who actually did the work), and Harold, who sat in the bows and played a medley of popular tunes on the accordion, his happy grin just visible above the instrument.

The aim of this ambitious voyage was to reach the basin beside Callis Mill, turn round and come back again (a journey that would probably have taken about ten minutes in the car). Soon Max took the strain and we were away. There were about thirty-five passengers, and we formed a pleasant friendly party. At the first lock the barge knocked somewhat violently against the side as the churning water lifted us up. A bit beyond I staggered down to the bar, and was rewarded with a half of lager and a nice smile from Emma.

We sailed on along the deep valley, the lush greens of the thickly wooded hillsides reflected in the still water. The banks on either side were ablaze with the blooms of yellow ragwort and rosebay willow herb, while the hanging baskets and window-boxes of the terraced cottages were full of geraniums, alyssum and lobelia. From the

* See Michael T. Greenwood, *The Rochdale: An Illustrated History of Trans-Pennine Canal Traffic* (privately published by Michael Greenwood, 18 Helston Drive, Royton, no date).

gardens we had quite a company of onlookers, mainly children, waving handkerchiefs as we sailed by at a very leisurely speed. Outside the Stubbing Wharf a quartet of very serious drinkers stolidly ignored us.

The supper trays were now handed out, and I got several envious glances when mine arrived, for the vegetarian special proved to be bigger and better than all the rest. It consisted of some sort of cheesy dumpling, with masses of vegetables.

Eventually we reached the wide basin at Callis Mill and turned round. A more convivial mood seemed to animate the return journey, as we sang along to Harold's renditions of 'There is a tavern in the town' and 'On Ilkley Moor baht 'at'. It was now getting dark and lights began to appear in the tall houses that stretch away up the hillsides above Hebden Bridge. We reached the marina and disembarked, giving Max a farewell pat as he returned to munching his hay.

14

Last Days at Thurstonland

While all this toing and froing went on, life in Thurstonland continued in its age-old rhythm. Yet I was aware that in various ways my bonds with the village were loosening. This was partly because I was spending more and more of my time at Todmorden – eventually half my life. There were also the ravages of the dark reaper. One winter I attended five funerals in quick succession. After each one I threw my black tie back in the drawer hoping it wouldn't be needed again, only to find myself fishing it out once more. I finally threw it back after the fifth such event, where strangely enough it has remained undisturbed.

Two of these deaths were of close Thurstonland friends: our next-door neighbour John Battye, whose fine bass-baritone voice had graced the village concerts, as well as more prestigious events, and Constance Adamson. Constance had come to the village about the time of my own arrival. She had married Ralph and settled down just round the corner. Like me, she had come to love the place, and would go for as many walks as her precarious health would permit, and gather all the interesting information she could discover. I think she vaguely envisaged writing a history of Thurstonland, but this never came to fruition.

One subject that greatly intrigued Constance was field names, and she would talk to the local farmers and make lists of their fields. This is an interesting approach, since field names often commemorate little bits of local history and mythology. In some cases the meanings were obvious, such as Tunnel Field or Church Field. But what about Hanging Royd Shrogg? Well, 'shrogg' apparently means a wood of stunted trees. Even more interesting was Old Maid's Field, so named because (for some unrecorded reason) the haymaking there was always done by two old maids wearing shirts and sun-bonnets. The village also had an Old Maid's Well, and tradition held that any girl who lingered beside it would remain a maid forever. Eventually the council (in its usual unheeding way) concreted it over. Whether they were worried about an excessive number of cases of prolonged virginity I don't know; I have no recollection of it being a serious problem.

The religious life of the community went through something of a renaissance while I was living there, and one sign of this was the revamping of the annual Christmas service. The first big problem was to warm up the church, and for many hours

A Thurstonland village concert, 4 April 1979. From left to right: the author, Milovan Jelic, Ralph Adamson, Anne Simpson and Geoffrey Hamilton. (Courtesy of the Huddersfield Examiner)

beforehand the heaters would be valiantly attempting to raise the temperature in the chilly corners of St Thomas's. Shortly after two the bell tolled, and almost everyone in the village – Anglicans, Catholics, Baptists, Druids, Agnostics, Heretics, even an occasional Methodist – forsook the comfort of their coal fires and came flocking to the church, so deeply buried were the ancient hostilities. Ralph and Constance would be at the door, dishing out the Bethlehem Carol Sheets, the Christmas tree (traditionally supplied by me) was lit, and everyone shuffled into the normally empty pews. Then there was that magical moment when Stephen, the principal choirboy, sang solo the first verse of 'Once in Royal David's City', and slowly the choir processed up the nave of the dimly lit church, each member holding a candle. Then the infants would sing 'The Little Fir Tree', John Battye's fine rich voice would give a rendition of 'Mary's Boy Child', and of course there were the usual readings and performances by the choir.

I don't remember that Thurstonland Church Choir was ever a particularly bright star in the Yorkshire musical firmament. (Indeed, the fact that I once sang with them suggests their standards were abysmally low.) However, we did enjoy performances of a much higher order at the classical concerts occasionally put on at the village school. Looking back at my notes about these, some rather unexpected items appear: one year Milovan Jelic performed on the vihuela, an ancestor of the guitar, while the 18-year-old Anne Simpson played a Hindemith violin sonata (was Thurstonland really ready for Hindemith? Presumably it was). Occasionally I got previews of some items, and I can remember the sounds of John Battye and Prabu Singh rehearsing the 'Hippopotamus Song' wafting over the garden wall.

Sometimes the whole village would act in unison for some practical activity. I can recall one very hot afternoon when it was decided we would all have a blitz on the very overgrown churchyard. In the bright merciless sunlight, sickles and scythes did battle with rosebay willow herb, milk thistles and other intruders; over-full wheelbarrows carted the refuse to a big heap in the far corner; and various ladies set up a stall by the church porch and plied us with tea. At the end of all the sweat and tears I was asked to write a poem to commemorate the battle. Regrettably I never did so – perhaps this brief mention can serve as a substitute.

The author taking part in the great tidying of Thurstonland churchyard. (Photograph: Michael Smith)

But all this was coming to an end – the toing and froing to Todmorden couldn't go on forever. Catherine and I talked over various plans for the future, but the only feasible one seemed to be for me to move to Todmorden. After twenty-three years at Thurstonland it was a big wrench, and nothing less exciting than a woman could have tempted me to do it.

And so the old process went into reverse. I entered Brian Turner's estate agents (where it had all begun), and asked for the house to be put on the market. Brian himself came over one dull December afternoon. He seemed in a most gloomy mood, and sat in a chair in the living room muttering pessimistic remarks about the state of the housing market. I began to think it would be another twenty-three years before I could sell the place. However, his despairing prognostications proved quite untrue. On the very last day of 1993 I had a phone call from a lady expressing interest. On 6 January she and her husband came, looked at the place and liked it. On the 8th an offer was made and accepted.

The move from Thurstonland, after so many years there, might have been very nostalgic. However, I was far too busy with the practicalities of the thing to have much time for reflection. Only on some of the late afternoon walks on the Heights with Sooty would I feel some sense of what I was losing, as the rooks flew in a great flock eastwards over Farnley Moor and the dusk gathered on the distant Pennines. And then of course there was the human loss: Ralph Adamson in particular. We spent a lot of time together during those last few weeks, going for short walks in the morning and for swims at Holmfirth in the afternoon.

But of course the main thing was the move itself, and all the jobs it triggered off. As we were merging the contents of two houses a lot of things had to go. The first thing was the piano, on which I had played indifferently since my teens. As I had had to saw its legs off and then put them back on again when moving in, I was somewhat apprehensive about this. I contacted Christopher Brown, a piano-dealer, and agreed on a price. Then we tried to get it into the hall. Halfway through it got stuck, and Christopher had to climb out of the window to check on the problem. After sawing off two small triangles of wood from the corners, we succeeded in pushing it into the hall. Next day two very jolly piano-shifters came and took it away. (I should think a sense of humour would be essential in that job.)

John Holmes, the local farmer and milkman, provided some comic relief. One afternoon he invited me along to his home to see his paintings. After we'd been talking for about an hour he suddenly asked if I'd be recommending his milk-round to the new people at my house. I replied that I was doubtful, as the milk came quite late in the day and in fact I'd considered changing myself. At this he was rather taken aback, and promised that for the remaining fortnight of my stay I would have my milk delivered personally by him on the previous evening some time before ten o'clock.

That evening I glanced at the front doorstep at 10.30 p.m. and could see no sign of the promised milk. I went to bed, and was just dozing off at about 11.15 p.m. when I heard a curious crashing sound, followed by Sooty barking furiously. I put on my dressing gown, descended the stairs, flung open the front door – and behold a pint of milk! When I phoned next morning to complain about being awakened, John explained that the crashing sound was caused by him tripping in the darkness, and falling headlong into the front garden. However, he proved as good as his word over the remaining deliveries, and I did in fact recommend him. We parted on good terms.

When it came to the actual move I didn't have far to look, as Tony Bowden, only two doors down, ran a removal service. The date was fixed for 23 February. During the previous night I was vaguely aware that it was snowing, but it wasn't until I looked out of the window next morning that I realised we had had the worst fall of the entire winter. I got up, had breakfast and took Sooty for a walk to the Heights. The snow was so deep that I was convinced the house-move was completely out of the question. But I returned home to find Tony gritting the roadway in a very determined mood: 'Oh, we're going to Todmorden – we're going to Todmorden today.' Jack Crookes turned up to disconnect the washer, full of his usual jokes and good humour. Keith Matthews likewise disconnected the cooker, and a couple of men arrived to read the gas and electric meters respectively. Meanwhile, Tony, Catherine and I had started to load up the big van, as Tony's assistant hadn't yet turned up.

It was a swine of a job carrying all the big pictures out of the door, down the steep drive and into the van with the snow blowing furiously across the path. John Holmes walked by and remarked that he and his family had moved to Thurstonland in a snowstorm seventy years ago. 'At least you had the sense to stay', was my reply.

Tony's assistant Alan now arrived, a very sturdy good-humoured gentleman. Things went better thereafter, with jokes flying almost as fast as the snowflakes. At last we were loaded, the big things in the van and the smaller items in my car. As we set off I was too focused on my driving to have time for nostalgia.

Now when I think of Thurstonland it isn't really that tangible place which I still sometimes visit to keep in touch with old friends. To some extent it's the view from the Pennines: the two low hills and the long saddle between. But in a sense it isn't even that: just the childish doodle, with the clump of trees and the tall church spire sticking up from their midst.

15

Todmorden

29 May 2004. At 5.30 a.m. I was awakened by the wind. I got up and parted the curtains. The morning was already bright; sunshine and shadow alternated on the moorland, and long streamers of greyish cloud moved steadily in the prevailing wind. I dressed and went downstairs, put on my walking boots and went out. The curious mild summer wind was strong enough to have scattered the petals of the horse chestnut flowers all over the track, and had even brought down a few minor branches as well. A female chaffinch flew up into an apple tree, while a jay squawked unseen from a sycamore. The paddock was full of buttercups swaying in the wind. Higher up rabbits scampered over the fields at 'Billy's Back'. I climbed up the heather-skirted path, and then turned left along the track known as Broad Gate. The hillsides were bright with spring-flowering gorse and broom; Rive Rocks, lying in shadow, looked dark and sombre by contrast. I went through the narrow gate and climbed to the top of the big lumpy millstone-grit rocks. Then I paused to admire the view.

It's a splendid scene from up here, with all the geography and history of the upper Calder Valley laid out beneath you. To the north-west is the blue-grey outline of Thievely Pike (just over the Lancashire border), and below it the Burnley Valley with its wooded slopes and ribbon development in the narrow bottom; to the south lies the valley of the Walsden Water with Dulesgate joining it from the north-west.

Through this gap in the hills between Todmorden and Littleborough (the lowest crossing of the Pennines south of the Aire Gap) run the great arteries of transport: the railway spanning Todmorden centre with an eight-arched viaduct and then disappearing somewhere beyond Walsden into Summit Tunnel; the Rochdale Canal, a short stretch glinting in the early morning sun, just visible near 'the Great Wall of Tod'; and the road, quite silent at this early hour.

In Todmorden itself the most conspicuous building is the Town Hall, its freshly cleaned white stone gleaming in the sunlight. Higher up, and less prominent in its uncleaned state, stands the Unitarian church, cathedral-like in its dimensions, and with a magnificent spire pointing upwards at the hurrying grey clouds. Up on the hillside to the west lies Dobroyd Castle, also uncleaned and difficult to spot against the background of dark woodland. These three buildings have one thing in common: they all owe their origin to the munificence of the Fielden family, whose rise and fall is linked with so much of Todmorden's history. And despite their very differing styles they all had the same architect – John Gibson. The once-vast mills which created the wealth have gone, but the products of that wealth remain.

The basic shape of Todmorden is somewhat like that of the 'spiders' one had to insert in the centre of some old-fashioned 45rpm records. Its houses, shops, pubs and small factories sprawl out from the centre in three directions, along the Burnley, Rochdale and Halifax Roads. Above the valley floor the steep sides are mostly wooded – mainly beech and oak – with the occasional scar of an ancient quarry. Above this is the 'shelf', a broad undulating area of farming land, its large fields dotted with sheep and cattle, with the odd farmhouse and even a few hamlets or small villages such as Sourhall, Lumbutts and Mankinholes. Higher still is the edge of the moorland and 'the Tops': Hoof Stones Height, Flower Scar Hill, Trough Edge, Langfield Common and Stoodley Pike. The latter is capped with the famous monument, the best-known landmark in the area.

When the history of Todmorden is mentioned one tends to think immediately of the industrial revolution, since its monuments are still very much around us. But there was human activity in the area long before this, not in the valley bottoms (which were swampy and difficult to cross), but on that broad undulating shelf. The most desirable part of the shelf was that which had a south-facing aspect, and it is here that the most significant ancient sites are to be found. Particularly important is the Blackheath Barrow, only a short distance from Rive Rocks, on what is now the sixth fairway of Todmorden Golf Course. It dates from the Bronze Age and was a burial place for the ashes of the departed. Some of the funeral urns are now on display in the public library.

Todmorden has always been on the borders of things. At one time the boundary of Yorkshire and Lancashire actually ran through the Town Hall, but this unhappy arrangement came to an end in 1888. The border is still close, and one gets the impression that the local inhabitants (technically in Yorkshire) are quite happy to enjoy any benefits which may accrue from being regarded as Lancastrians. In the Middle Ages Todmorden lay at the meeting point of three townships, Stansfield, Hundersfield and Langfield. No big residential lord or baron imposed his will on the immediate area, and until the fifteenth century there was no church, the nearest ones being at Heptonstall and Rochdale. Thus a certain independence of outlook developed which can be seen continuing throughout the town's history – witness in particular the opposition to the Poor Law in the mid-nineteenth century. Perhaps the occasional bursts of aggression between the town council and the local authority can be seen as rumblings in a very ancient tradition.

Up until the early sixteenth century the predominant activity was of course agriculture. Then, somewhere about 1520, a dual economy developed with the rise of the so-called yeoman clothier. Why this happened isn't immediately obvious. The acidic boggy moorland soil was by no means ideal for sheep rearing, and the area had poor access to both markets and raw material. One reason sometimes given is that it was customary for a landowner to divide his property among all his sons. Thus farms became more and more fragmented, and the inheritors of these small farms had to look for another source of income. Wool-spinning and weaving seemed the obvious choice, even though some of the raw wool had to be brought into the valley from as far afield as Lincolnshire.

As the cottage-based textile industry developed, it became apparent that the locality had one great asset: a plentiful supply of water power, not just on the main rivers like the Calder and the Walsden Water, but also on those swiftly descending streams that rush down the small tributary valleys, Colden Clough, Lumbutts Clough and Jumble Hole. Of course the use of water power went back to the Middle Ages, and it had long been used for corn mills and fulling mills. The adaptation to more sophisticated branches of the textile process was an obvious development. Soon the fast tributary streams were driving the small 'overshot' water-wheels, while the main rivers rotated the bigger 'undershot' versions. When steam power came it did not immediately replace water power. It is often forgotten that in lots of mills the two forms of power worked in combination for many years.

It was clear that if the textile industry of the upper Calder Valley was going to expand, the transport system would have to be much improved. For many years packhorses had been the main means of transporting goods, not just carrying the finished cloth to market at Halifax, but also bringing in coal for the steam boilers. The remains of the well-worn packhorse tracks can still be seen crossing the hillsides above Mankinholes and beneath Whirlaw Rocks. But much better roads were obviously needed. In the 1760s turnpike roads were opened between Halifax and Todmorden, Todmorden and Burnley, and Todmorden and Rochdale. The finest memento of these early roads is the splendid hexagonal Toll House at Steanor Bottom, where one can still read that the passage of a calf, sheep, swine or lamb will cost a farthing, and that of an ox or cow one ha'penny, while a horse drawing a landau, chariot or chase would cost the princely sum of 7*d*.

Plans to build a canal up the valley were at first opposed by the mill owners, who feared that their precious water supply would be jeopardised as water was diverted into the canal. However, a compromise was arrived at, and in 1794 Parliament gave its approval. The canal was built to cross the Pennines without the use of a tunnel; its highest point, the appropriately named 'Summit', lay at 600ft. It uses one of the lowest possible crossings of the Pennines, but none the less it required thirty-six locks on the eastern side and fifty-six on the western. The water was supplied by the large reservoirs on Blackstone Edge Moor and by Hollingworth 'Lake' – actually a big reservoir. The so-called Rochdale Canal was finally opened in 1804.

The last important development in transport was the coming of the railway. Not surprisingly, this was opposed by the Rochdale Canal Company, and the first proposal in 1831 was defeated. But in 1836 Parliament gave its approval, and work began in August 1837. The narrow valley already contained the turnpike road and the canal, and the construction of a railway was quite an engineering challenge. Several tunnels were involved, the longest being the Summit Tunnel, which for a few months held the record as the longest railway tunnel in the world. There were also some spectacular viaducts, notably the nineteen arches of Gauxholme Viaduct and the magnificent eight-arch viaduct that strides proudly across Todmorden town centre. The entire line was open for trains by March 1841. One of the new railway's early employees was Branwell Brontë, brother of the more famous sisters, who worked at Sowerby Bridge and Luddendenfoot. But his place in the history of railways is even smaller than his one in the history of art and literature, for after a year and a half he was dismissed for gross neglect of his duties.

This brief account of transport development in the area has taken us forward in time. We must go back almost a hundred years in order to trace the fortunes of Todmorden's most famous business dynasty, the Fieldens. Of course there were other significant manufacturing families, among them the Ormerods, the Crossleys and the Greenwoods. But the name Fielden has come to sum up the industrial revolution in the minds of most local people thanks to their spectacular rise to power, the great buildings they created and their work as radical reformers. One of their members, 'Honest John', has a place not just in local history but in national history.

The story starts with Joshua Fielden, who was born in 1748 at Edge End Farm, which still stands on the hillside overlooking the Walsden Valley. He was a Quaker, and would seem in his early days to have been a typical yeoman clothier, the cloth he dealt with at this time being woollen. In 1772 he married Jenny Greenwood, and rapidly set to work begetting a large family. He must, however, have been ambitious, for in 1782 he borrowed money from some Quaker friends and bought three cottages at Laneside. Like Edge End Farm, they are all still inhabited. Only a small part of the premises was for living in, the rest became a miniature cotton mill. It did well, and by the time of Joshua's death in 1811 Joshua Fielden & Sons was a small struggling company similar to several others in the Calder Valley.

The meteoric rise to power came with the next generation, when the firm changed its name to Fielden Brothers. There were five brothers, Samuel, Joshua, John ('Honest John'), James and Thomas. During these years vast quantities of cheap cotton clothing were being sold to both the home market and abroad – particularly India. But it was not all smooth going for the industry, since booms were frequently followed by depressions, when many firms went out of business. The fact that Fielden Brothers not only survived but prospered seems to have been due to three main factors: the close cooperation between the five brothers; the outstanding leadership qualities of the third son, John; and the policy of clinging on to the workforce during periods of depression, so that the firm was fully prepared when the next boom came along.

'Honest John' Fielden is the central figure in the history of the Fieldens; in fact in most ways he is the central figure in the history of Todmorden. He received a somewhat curious education from a local character known as 'Long Sam'. This gentleman was himself illiterate, but managed to train his pupils by getting them to read out items from the radical *Leeds Mercury* and then leading a discussion on what they had read. How an illiterate man could teach his pupils to read in the first place is difficult to imagine. However, the end result seems to have been a group of boys who could not only read and write, but also expound revolutionary politics. When Joshua realised with horror what was happening, he abruptly took John away from the influence of Long Sam and put him to work in the cotton mill. But the

'Honest John' Fielden from the portrait by John Bostock in the Bankfield Museum, Halifax. (Photograph: Mark Croft, courtesy of Calderdale Council, Libraries, Museums and Arts)

conditioning of his teacher lived on in him. Nor did he forget the exhaustion he felt after working many weary hours in his father's mill while still only 10 years old, even although conditions there were relatively mild compared to some other mills.

John vividly remembered this early background, and it shaped his later life. A man of prodigious energy, he made an impact in several fields, both locally and nationally. In matters of religion he soon tired of the 'quietist' attitude of contemporary Quakerism. After experiments with Methodism and Anglicanism he finally found in Unitarianism an attitude of mind that chimed in with his deepest feelings. His change of religion affected his work as an educationalist, and many well-known citizens of later years owed their early training to his Unitarian classrooms. Furthermore he and his brothers set up factory schools close to their mills at Waterside, Robinwood and Lumbutts. In the realm of politics he became the Liberal

MP for Oldham. He is mainly remembered for the Ten Hours' Bill, but he was also a great opponent of the Poor Law and was a principal speaker at the big Yorkshire Chartist gatherings. John Bostock's portrait of John Fielden portrays him resting his head on his right hand in thoughtful mood; beneath his bushy eyebrows, his eyes suggest both intelligence and benevolence.

Alma Dawson looking after four looms in the weaving shed at Albion Mill, Todmorden, 1943. This stretch was popularly known as 'Glamour Alley'. (Photograph: Enoch Horsfall, courtesy of Roger Birch)

Mrs Eastwood working on a ring-spinning frame at Mons Mill, Todmorden, 1948. (Photograph: Enoch Horsfall, courtesy of Roger Birch)

The age of 'Honest John' represented the high point in the history of the Fieldens. One feels something of a step downwards in coming to the next generation, which was dominated by John's three sons, Samuel, John (junior) and Joshua. However, it was in their lifetime that Todmorden's famous Fielden buildings were erected: the magnificent Town Hall, the Unitarian church, Dobroyd Castle (now owned by a Buddhist group), the Fielden Centre and Stansfield Hall. The eldest son Samuel (1816–89) seems to have concealed a secret benevolence beneath a bleak exterior. Those who saw only the outside nicknamed him 'Black Sam'. Something of a local legend has gathered around the early life of the second son John. He fell in love with the beautiful Ruth Stansfield, a farmer's daughter who worked with her sisters at the local mill. They used to frequent the pathway beneath Buckley Wood which is known to this day as 'Lovers' Walk', and modern couples amble along it hand in hand in honour of the great tradition. Sadly the marriage of John and Ruth eventually foundered. They were childless, and Ruth found upper-class living a great strain. She took to drink and spent her last years away from Dobroyd Castle (which John had had specially built for her) at the so-called 'Swiss Chalet', where she died in 1877. John remarried with somewhat unseemly haste, and further disgraced the family by becoming an Anglican. The third son Joshua lived much of his life at Stansfield Hall, although he later tired of Todmorden and moved to Nutfield Priory in Surrey. He married Ellen Brocklehurst, and they had thirteen children. Like his father, Joshua became an MP (as a Conservative!), and spent much of his time agitating over the Malt Tax – surely a trivial affair compared to the great causes espoused by his father.

The glory fades even further with the next generation. Joshua's second son Edward was persuaded to become chairman of Fielden Brothers, although most of the family wealth went to 'Black Sam's' only child John Ashton Fielden. Eventually the cousins quarrelled, and this further undermined the firm's fortunes. Quite apart from this, the British cotton industry was itself in decline. Rightly and inevitably, the countries to which Fieldens had once exported vast quantities of cheap cloth had built up their own industries, and no longer needed to import.

During its last years the firm was under the control of Edward's second son Nicholas. It ceased to trade as Fielden Brothers in 1966, and changed, both in name and in activity, to Waterside Plastics. This finally closed in 1990. However, the name is by no means dead. The local telephone directory lists sixty-three Fieldens, and every so often there is a grand reunion, with Fieldens coming from all over the world. Occasionally on my walks through Centre Vale Park I meet old Jacob Fielden, a direct descendant of the great 'Honest John'. Although now over 90, he climbs Stoodley Pike every year on his birthday. The spirit of endeavour lives on!

I have perhaps dwelt overlong on the Fieldens, as if their history was the entire story of Todmorden. However, in a short study such as this, their fortunes have had to stand for much else. There were of course plenty of other employers with busy mills – Mons Mill, Albion Mill and many more. Likewise I should have mentioned the famous people the town has produced: the naturalists John Nowell and Abraham Stansfield; the poets Sam Law and James Standing; the popular band-leader Geoff Love; the writer, artist and noted eccentric Billy Holt; and the two Nobel Laureates Sir John Cockcroft and Sir Geoffrey Wilkinson. But in a sense the cotton industry was the background to everything else. In my early years in Todmorden, my morning walk with Sooty would usually take us past the premises of the Cinderhill Spinning Company, Todmorden's last textile firm. Alas, even this has now closed.

It was a strange experience going shopping in Todmorden during those early days. Everyone seemed to know everyone else, and I knew no one. In fact, not only did they know each other, but they seemed to have done so since childhood, and could even tell you whether their maternal great-grandmother was a Cockcroft or a Crabtree.

Little by little things improved. My first contacts were with the local dog-walkers, usually comments shouted from a safe distance, for Sooty was a great fighter. From such exchanges I learnt the dog's breed, age and name, and was occasionally even privileged enough to learn the name of its owner. There were other occasions for socialising. I took to visiting the local swimming pool for a swim before breakfast every Sunday morning. There were always the three of us standing waiting when Carol struggled to unlock the door: Russell, Jack and me. Jack's lively anecdotes in the gents' changing room were an essential part of the experience. The place was in a dilapidated state; the tiles were peeling off the walls and the pool leaked and had to be topped up with a cold hose. Loud vulgar music played as we swam up and down – the sort of thing that would have made me scream at other times, but seemed quite enjoyable in the circumstances. Eventually the establishment was pulled down, and for five years Todmorden didn't have a swimming pool. Finally a new sports centre was opened, with a smart new swimming pool. I went along before breakfast on the first Sunday it was open, and there were Jack and Russell standing around as if the intervening years had never happened.

There are few better ways of developing a feeling of belonging to a place than taking an interest in its history. Catherine was already a member of the Todmorden Antiquarian Society, and I started going along to meetings with her. They were held in the court room at the Town Hall, and were always well attended. In fact I had never lived in a place which had such a strong interest in its past. The attendance was at least equal to that of the corresponding society in Huddersfield, despite the fact that Todmorden is only one-tenth the size, and the degree of enthusiasm was at least ten times greater. Minute details of the town's history would be hotly debated, such as whether Sam Law the poet and Sam Law the schoolmaster were one and the same person. The meetings were chaired by an enthusiastic little man named Dennis O'Neill, a former Town Mayor who was blessed with a wealth of local knowledge. There was something about his mannerisms which seemed familiar, and eventually it dawned on me that it was he who had given the talk about local architecture on that memorable evening at Mankinholes Hostel when I was walking the Pennine Way.

Getting ready for the Todmorden Carnival, Industrial Street, 1985. (Photograph: Roger Birch)

As Thomas Moore (the poet, not the saint) once said: 'Coming events cast their shadows before.'

I want to end this rather fragmentary portrait of Todmorden with a scene from the annual Carnival. The moments I find most evocative are not the procession down Halifax Road, nor the dancing and acrobatics which take place later in Centre Vale Park, but the assembling and warming-up before the procession begins. It takes place in a group of grey, superficially dreary streets, which date back to the late nineteenth century. Industrial Street, Sackville Street, Anchor Street, Hazlewood Street and various others are low lying, and are always among the first to flood when the Calder bursts its banks. They were built for the local workers in the cotton mills, and have no doubt housed many generations of spinners, tacklers and weavers. Somehow they were lucky enough to have escaped the great demolition craze of the 1960s, and are now deemed to have a special beauty all of their own.

The build-up starts at about noon. Various big lorries manoeuvre round the awkward corners, their sides brightly decorated. These floats mainly of course represent local firms, but there is one small street down by the canal, Erringden

Street, which has a float all of its own. (I gather the inhabitants celebrate with a party into the early hours.) Then there are the foot tableaux, perhaps representing a famous character such as Elvis Presley. The balloon-sellers seem in danger of being carried high above the Calder Valley. A little girl sits on a brown pony; wearing a tall pointed hat and a red and white flowing dress, she attempts to re-create the age of chivalry. But most fascinating of all are the drum majorettes. They take advantage of the time in hand, and form up in the middle of Industrial Street to rehearse their exercises. They are in their early teens and full of energy, wearing mauve tops, short red and white skirts, and brown stockings, and holding white pom-poms in their hands. Their arms start moving in rhythm, the pom-poms dance against the grey walls – youth, symbolising both the present and the future, enlivening the half-memory of an ancient past.

Postscript

Thursday 24 November 2005, 3.15 p.m. I write this in my sketch pad, seated on a rock high above Hill House Clough on a cold but sunny early winter afternoon. Despite it being so late, the autumn tints are at their best – the beeches in the wood beyond the clough are a vivid orange-russet, glowing in the warm light as the sun slides down to Trough Edge. Black-faced sheep graze on the steady slopes, and four big horses, wrapped in their warm blue coats, make the most of things on the shadowy side of the valley. On the canal some children splash the oars of a canoe, their shrieks of delight clearly audible from afar. The traffic rumbles on the Todmorden–Halifax road; the odd train crosses Horsfall Viaduct; the Hill House Beck gurgles somewhere in the depths below me.

I started this book in August 1994. Why has it taken me so long to write a mere fifteen chapters? Really, I'm not sure. Interruptions, perhaps? But maybe this is merely an excuse. The plain fact is that eleven years have elapsed since I started it. Much has happened in those eleven years. Catherine and I got married on the morning of 1 September 1994 at a very quiet ceremony in Richmond (Richmond in Yorkshire, that is). That afternoon there was a concert of fifteenth-century music in the grounds of Richmond Castle, which we attended in the company of my son Robert. There were only two musicians, yet they managed between them to play at least nine instruments, including bagpipes, a harp, a three-holed pipe, nackers (whatever they are), a hurdy gurdy, a medieval trumpet, a bell and a rebec. As we sat there on the small, rather hard, wooden benches, all three of us felt that it had been put on specially for us.

Sooty had come with us on our very brief honeymoon, and joined us in a walk by the River Swale that evening, the late sunlight shining benignly on the waterfalls and fine stone bridges. (Was this really the same place I had seen snowbound on that first day in the army thirty-nine years ago?) Next day we visited Jervaulx Abbey, surely the very epitome of a romantic ruin, with the crevices of its crumbling walls filled with wild flowers. Then came the long drive home across the Yorkshire Dales, through Wensleydale and Nidderdale, with distant views of the blue-grey outline of the hills – Great Whernside, Little Whernside and many more.

Catherine had worked in banking all her life, but eventually switched profession and became town clerk of Todmorden. Now she copes with the challenges of small-town politics, both the aggro and the humour. In her spare time she pursues her interests in local history, needlecrafts and antiques. My time is mainly divided between four activities: walking, swimming, writing and painting, although I also enjoy somewhat mundane chores such as ironing and washing-up. The more creative side of my life brings its successes and disappointments. As far as the visual arts are concerned, for some years I devoted a lot of time to exhibitions. Eventually I came to the conclusion that it brought more trouble than reward, and am now content that my work should be known through postcards and book illustrations.

Writing likewise has its ups and downs. Many of the recent 'ups' have been linked with the intense interest which Catherine and I feel for the Brontë sisters, both their lives and their writings. Some of our work has been published jointly, but even the writings attributed to me alone have involved a tremendous amount of help from Catherine. In May 2004 we led the Brontë Society's annual walk, and followed a route round the Cross Stone area of Todmorden, associated with the sisters' great-uncle, the Revd John Fennell. During the walk Bob Duckett, the honorary publication secretary of the Society, asked us to write an article about this reverend gentleman, and it was while researching this that we accidentally came across George Sowden's *Recollections of the Brontës*. These reminiscences, written in his old age by the younger brother of Sutcliffe Sowden, who had officiated at the wedding of Charlotte Brontë and Arthur Bell Nicholls, had lain virtually forgotten for over a hundred years. Their publication in May 2005 proved to be the first success in what turned out to be a bit of a 'hat-trick'. It was followed by the long article on John Fennell in the July issue of *Brontë Studies*, and only recently saw the launch of my book *Pilgrims from Loneliness: An Interpretation of Charlotte Brontë's* Jane Eyre *and* Villette. Like the present piece of writing, it had been drafted out long ago, and polished and repolished over the years.

To counterbalance all this there were the disappointments and frustrations. Three prose novels drew from the publishers nothing but a pile of rejection slips. (Bohuslav Barlow and I once contemplated having an exhibition of rejection slips – we thought it might win the Turner Prize!) Strangely enough the only novel of mine to be accepted was a novel-in-verse entitled *Pirouette of Earth*, but it has sold very slowly, most people finding the idea of a novel told entirely in poetry extremely odd. As for my collections of shorter poems, I have had to contend with the British public's ambivalent attitude to poetry as described at the beginning of chapter 8. Ultimately there is only one thing to do in life: one must plod on, making the most of successes but accepting failures with as much resignation as one can muster.

Little by little I have come to love Todmorden, even if a certain yearning for the village where I lived for twenty-three years remains. I go back to Thurstonland every so often to visit various old friends. It doesn't change much – a few new houses,

nothing more. Does the church bell still get clogged up with pigeon excreta? I don't know. Perhaps they have blocked up the holes.

I am now just 69 and so officially an old age pensioner. I have collected my bus-pass, but not used it yet. My mother lived to be 95, and was clear in her mind to the end. Have I another twenty-six years? I rather hope so, for there are many things in life I still want to do.

The sun is just touching Trough Edge. A kestrel, seemingly unaware of my presence, hovers close by. The children in the canoe have screamed themselves hoarse and come ashore. The valley fills with shadow, but the moors around Stoodley Pike are still bathed in winter sunlight.

Bibliography

Barlow, Bohuslav, *Visual Alchemy*, text by Jeff Nuttall, introduction by John Robert-Blunn (Babylon Trust, 1987)

Brown, Fred, *The Muse Went Weaving* (Hub Publications and the Yorkshire Dialect Society, 1972)

Browning, L. and Senior, R.K., *The Old Yards of Huddersfield* (Huddersfield Civic Society, 1986)

Croft, Linda, *John Fielden's Todmorden* (Tygerfoot Press, 1994)

Edwards, Robert, *And the Glory: A History in Commemoration of the 150th Anniversary of the Huddersfield Choral Society* (Maney, 1985)

Eyre, Kathleen, *The Real Lancashire* (Dalesman Books, 1983)

Goodes, Agnes, 'The Poor Law in Thurstonland, 1775 to 1834' (1997), typescript in Huddersfield Library Archives Department KX 379

Graham, Sir James, *A Guide to Norton Conyers* (no publication details given on author's copy)

Greenwood, Michael, *The Rochdale: An Illustrated History of Trans-Pennine Canal Traffic* (privately published by Michael Greenwood, 18 Helston Drive, Royton, no date)

Grove, Sir George, *Dictionary of Music* (articles on Sir Walter Parratt, Sir Edward Bairstow, Joseph Holbrooke and Eaglefield Hull)

Hammerton, J.A. (ed.), *Wonderful Britain*, 4 vols (Fleetway House, no date)

Hammond, David, 'Making Headway with the Gods', *Huddersfield Examiner*, 23 October 1990, p. 10

Heywood, Malcolm and Freda, and Jennings, Bernard, *A History of Todmorden*, with special illustrations by Lawrence Greenwood (Smith Settle, 1996)

Hill, Brian Merrikin, *Wakeful in the Sleep of Time* (Taxvs, 1984)

Hughes, Ted, *Remains of Elmet*, with photographs by Fay Godwin (Faber, 1979)

Law, Brian, *Fieldens of Todmorden: A Nineteenth-century Business Dynasty* (George Kelsall, 1995)

Lord, Mary, *Mary Lord: An Appreciation*, with text by John Sheeran and foreword by Alexander Robertson (Sheeran Lock, 1992)

Morehouse, Henry James, *The History and Topography of the Parish of Kirkburton and the Graveship of Holme including Holmfirth in the County of York* (self-published, 1861. Reprinted with an introduction by George Redmonds, 1984)

Parker, Denzil (ed.), *Memories of Thurstonland and Stocksmoor* (St Thomas's Church Committee, 2000)

Reader's Digest, *Complete Atlas of the British Isles* (The Reader's Digest Association, no date)

Smith, Ken Edward, *West Yorkshire Dialect Poets* (Dialect Books, 1982)

Sneyd, Steve, *The Cambodunum Chapbook Companion* (Hill Top Press, 1991)

Sowden, George, *Recollections of the Brontës* (Angria Press, 2005)

Todmorden Antiquarian Society, *Todmorden Cameos: People of Note from a Small Northern Town – A Millennium Celebration*, illustrated by Dennis O'Neill (Todmorden Antiquarian Society, 1999)

Turner, Whiteley, *A Spring-time Saunter Round and About Brontë Land*, 3rd edn (Halifax Courier, 1913, reprinted by Rigg, 1986)

Wainwright, Alfred, *A Pennine Way Companion* (Westmorland Gazette, 1968)

Wyles, David, *The Buildings of Huddersfield: Four Architectural Walks*, illustrated by David Wyles and John Charlton (Kirklees Metropolitan Council, no date)

Index